First edition September 2009

10 9 8 7 6 5 4 3 2 1

Visit our website: **www.titanbooks.com**

ACKNOWLEDGEMENTS

Titan Books would like to thank the cast and crew of *Heroes*, in particular Tim Kring and Jeph Loeb, who gave up their valuable time for the interviews included in this book. Thanks also to Neysa Gordon, Miriam Koch and Steve Coulter at NBC Universal. And, for their contributions to this book, thanks must go to Tara Bennett (pp171-174), Abbie Bernstein (pp18-25, 36-42, 66-73, 74-77, 94-97, 98-100, 101-102, 116-124, 130-136, 138-143, 144-151, 152-157, 158-164), Jake Black (pp103-107), Bryan Cairns (pp11-16, 52-59, 78-85), Paul Simpson (pp30-35), K. Stoddard Hayes (pp26-29, 44-51, 60-65, 108-115, 126-129, 165-170) and Owen Van Spall (pp4-10), and to Martin Eden and Zoe Hedges.

To receive advance information, news, competitions, and exclusive Titan offers online, please register as a member by clicking the "sign up" button on our website: **www.titanbooks.com** Did you enjoy this book? We love to hear from our readers. Please e-mail us at: **readerfeedback@titanemail.com** or write to Reader Feedback at the above address.

A CIP catalogue record for this title is available from the British Library.

Printed and bound in China by C & C Offset Printing Co, Ltd.

CONTENTS

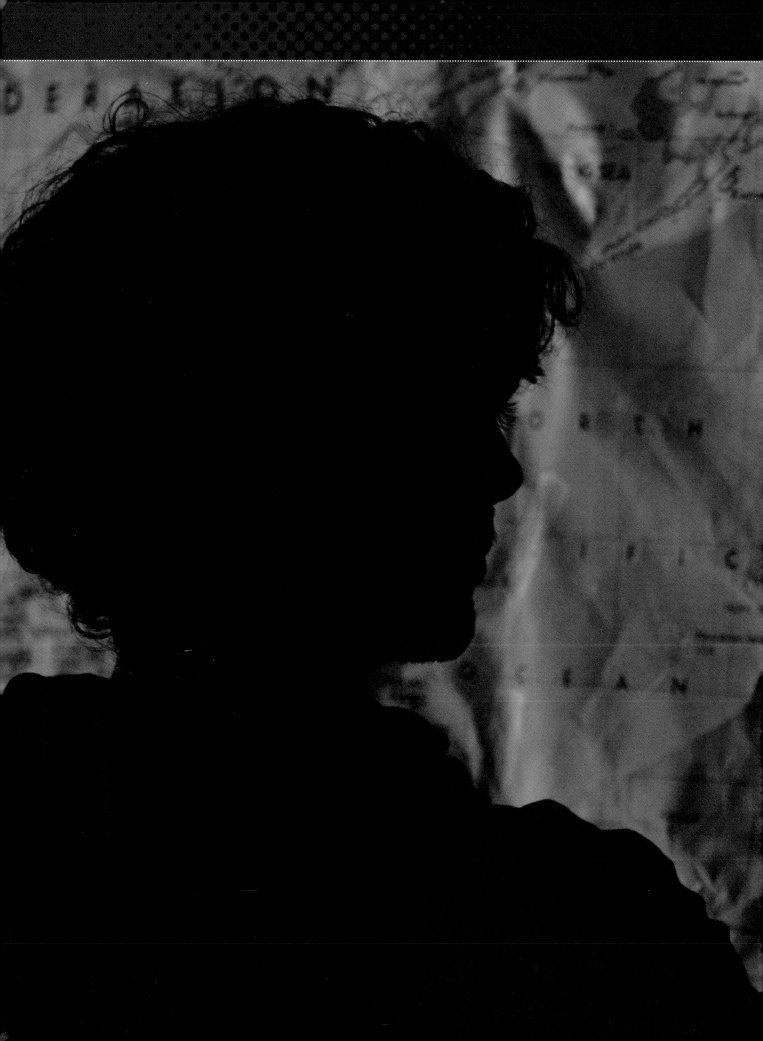

IN THE BEGINNING

A LOOK AT SEASON ONE, CHAPTER ONE: 'GENESIS'

MOHINDER'S MONOLOGUE:
"Where does it come from – this quest, this need to so
questions can never be answered? Why are we her
Perhaps we'd be better off not looking at
not human nature. Not the human hea

SYNOPSIS

Nurse Peter Petrelli has been having some seriously
strange dreams lately... about flying from a rooftop.
When he confides in his older brother, political candidate
and all-round cynic Nathan, he scoffs at them.

Across the world in Madras, India, genetics
professor Mohinder Suresh finds out his scientist dad
Chandra was killed whilst driving a taxi in New York
City. Mohinder visits his apartment, where he finds his
research files and a notated map. Hearing someone
in the next room, he makes a quick exit...

In Las Vegas, Niki Sanders, who earns money as
a stripper on the internet, notices her reflection move
independently as she passes a mirror. When two
thugs come to her front door looking to collect on a
debt, she grabs her young son Micah and runs.

Over in Odessa, Texas, cheerleader Claire
Bennet has her friend, Zach, film her. No, not for an
America's Next Top Model audition tape, but jumping
off a deserted oil-refinery tower. Popping back her
dislocated shoulder and pushing in some protruding
ribs after she lands, Claire seems to be indestructible,
but says Zach can't tell anyone, or even keep the
tape. Walking home, Claire and Zach come across
a trainwreck and Claire immediately runs into the
blaze, rescuing a man who's trapped inside.

In Tokyo, Japan, office drone Hiro Nakamura is
clock-watching in his cubicle. His stare grows more
and more intense, until suddenly the second hand

"...life's mysteries, when the simplest of
What is the soul? Why do we dream?
Not delving, not yearning. But that's
That is not why we are here..."

THE PAINTER'S HAND

In *Genesis*, Peter and Simone head to Isaac's apartment, where they find him reeling from an overdose. However, in the unaired pilot version (explained overleaf), Peter and Simone find that Isaac has cut off his own hand to get free from a radiator that he'd handcuffed himself to. This pretty graphic moment never made it into *Genesis*, as the writing team felt it was too debilitating an injury for a major character to have to recover from throughout the rest of season one.

EPISODE STATS:

EPISODE TITLE: Chapter One: *Genesis*
SEASON: One
FIRST US TRANSMISSION: 25 September, 2006
WRITTEN BY: Tim Kring
DIRECTED BY: David Semel
CAST:
Santiago Cabrera as Isaac Mendez
Tawny Cypress as Simone Deveaux
Noah Gray–Cabey as Micah Sanders
Ali Larter as Niki Sanders
Masi Oka as Hiro Nakamura
Hayden Panettiere as Claire Bennet
Adrian Pasdar as Nathan Petrelli
Sendhil Ramamurthy as Mohinder Suresh
Milo Ventimiglia as Peter Petrelli
Cristine Rose as Angela Petrelli
Jack Coleman as Mr. Bennet
Ashley Crowe as Sandra Bennet
James Kyson Lee as Ando Masahashi
Thomas Dekker as Zach
Shishir Kurup as Nirand
John Prosky as Principal
Deirdre Quinn as Tina
Brian Tarantina as Weasel
Richard Roundtree as Charles Deveaux
Randall Bentley as Lyle Bennet

moves one second back. Howling with joy ("Yatta!"), Hiro attempts to convince his friend and fellow geek, Ando, that he has the power to manipulate the space-time continuum. Trying to prove he really has superpowers, he first teleports into a ladies' restroom in a bar and later, on his own, teleports out of a Tokyo subway, right into the middle of Times Square, New York. He did it!

Meanwhile, Niki is laying low at her friend Tina's house, and tells her she borrowed $30,000 from a Mr. Linderman and is late repaying it. Returning to her house, Niki is attacked by Linderman's heavies, but blacks out. Later, she wakes up to find the thugs have been literally torn limb from limb in her now corpse-strewn garage. In a mirror, her bloody reflection gestures to her to be silent...

Artist Isaac Mendez is wrecking some of his paintings in his New York studio when his girlfriend Simone Deveaux walks in. Isaac says he doesn't remember painting several of them, and that he's been shooting up heroin. He shows Simone a painting of a bus on fire, which he says he painted three weeks ago. Then he shows her a picture in that morning's paper, of the same burning bus in Israel...

Peter catches a cab driven by Mohinder, who's in New York to continue his father's research and find his killer. As Peter gets out of the cab, another man gets in and notices Mohinder's license. He says that he knew a Professor Suresh once. An alarmed

Mohinder bolts from the cab. The man gets out – the same horn-rimmed glasses-wearing man who was in Chandra's apartment and who just so happens to be Claire Bennet's dad.

Simone and Peter find Isaac has OD'ed. Simone calls 911, but Peter is distracted by a painting – showing Peter flying from a roof. Peter and Simone then notice a huge floor-painting of a mushroom cloud over New York.

Peter calls his brother to an alley, calling to him from the edge of a roof. As Peter jumps, it's *Nathan* who flies, saving *him*... ▷

A NEW BEGINNING! THE PILOT THAT NEVER WAS…

"Every story has a beginning," the epic text crawl at the beginning of *Genesis* tells us. *Heroes* in fact has had more than one…

As the result of creative decisions (rather than Hiro's manipulations of the space-time continuum), the *Heroes* episode that first aired on US television in September 2006 – *Genesis* – was not the only *Heroes* pilot created. What became *Genesis* was actually an edited-down version of a longer "unaired pilot." This change would result in some major characters being introduced later

than originally intended, and some characters being removed from the series entirely.

Previously shown only once at the 2006 Comic-Con, fans worldwide are finally able to see the unaired 72–minute long pilot in its entirety on the *Heroes* season one DVD, complete with a revealing commentary by creator Tim Kring. Here we look at some of the key differences between the two versions – the aired pilot that forms the official, aired version will be referred to as *Genesis,* as compared to the "unaired pilot."

- Although they appear in the unaired pilot, Leonard Roberts and Greg Grunberg's characters, D.L. Hawkins and Matt Parkman, didn't make it into the final TV version. At NBC's Television Critics Association Event in 2006, *Heroes* creator and executive producer Tim Kring explained: "We shot a two-hour pilot. There were some story reasons why we cut it down. But, for the most part, we felt that an hour was about the limit for a screening."

- The pilot episode starts with all the characters scattered randomly over the globe. Tim Kring remarked at the Television Critics Association event on this set-up of a disparate group who must unite to save the world: "One of the things I wanted to do was start a show at the very beginning, to create a saga that literally started at the inception of when people discovered these things about themselves… It's kind of illogical to see that they would come together that quickly."

- As we all know, Masi Oka's portrayal of Hiro became one of the breakout characters in the pilot episode, and the character received a great reaction in the early showings and test screenings. However, Tim Kring revealed at the Television Critics Association event that he hadn't originally written Hiro Nakamura into the original pilot episode. Hiro was only added when it was decided that the show would benefit from a character who, unlike most of the others, actually got a kick out of his abilities.

- When Mohinder holds up a photo of his father in his Madras office, it doesn't feature Erick Avari, who eventually took the role. This was corrected when Avari was cast.

- Peter and Nathan's scenes in the campaign office were all shot in downtown Los Angeles, as is typical for *Heroes*. The Los Angeles exteriors in *Heroes* are dressed to resemble downtown New York City, complete with buses, yellow taxicabs, and extras.

- The Madras, India scenes were filmed on the Universal Studios back-lot, near Tim Kring's office, with many Madras interiors shot on the set of *Crossing Jordan*, a show Tim Kring also created.

- Mr. Bennet's now iconic horn-rimmed glasses make their first appearance here in Mohinder's father's apartment. The glasses were chosen from about 50 possible pairs!

- Much of Hiro's cubicle-filled office was created using CGI to enhance the drone-like feel, placing Hiro in an endless sea of cubicles. The set was only a tenth as large as it appears on screen.

- The scene where Niki confronts the Principal at Micah's school was the actual audition scene for the role of Niki Sanders itself (which we all know now was eventually won by Ali Larter).

- A lot of thought went into choosing Peter's coat – it's supposed to resemble a billowing superhero-style cape when he tries to fly off the roof and in Isaac's comic-book painting.

- The issue of *X-Men* Hiro mentions, #143, does not actually contain the Kitty Pryde story he refers to. He meant *Days of Future Past*, which appears in issues #141 and #142. Tim Kring has admitted the writers just got it wrong. 'Nuff said!

- The train cars used in the scene where Claire makes her daring rescue had to be returned in exactly the same state as they had been loaned, so all the fire effects used had to be carefully controled. The scenes where Hayden Panettiere enters the burning train car itself were almost not filmed because of budget constraints.

MEET MATT PARKMAN

Probably the biggest difference in the unaired pilot is the appearance of Matt Parkman. When the series aired on TV, his character wasn't introduced until the second episode, *Don't Look Back*. In the unaired pilot, Parkman's abilities manifest when he's drawn into the investigation of a terrorist cell. As the terrorist arc was removed from the *Genesis* pilot due to network concerns over its controversial nature, Matt Parkman's character was cut too (although elements of his original storyline were later worked into the aired season).

The first sign of the terrorist story, which ultimately ties into the train crash, can be seen in the unaired pilot as Claire and Zach walk back from their video shoot. A truck drives past them with some suspicious balaclava-clad men aboard.

Matt Parkman is on the scene of an investigation into a suspected terrorist cell in a South Central Los Angeles house. FBI agents search the house, but find no trace of "the engineer," Amid Halebi, a wanted terrorist. Matt's new telepathic powers run wild, but help him to locate

a member of the terrorist cell hiding under a floor grate. This earns him the attention of the FBI agent in charge (as occurs in episode two, *Don't Look Back* – although Clea DuVall, who played Agent Audrey Hanson, was cast later).

Meanwhile, Amid Halebi is taken to the cell leader, Joseph, who tells him he wants to cause an explosion using a device taken from the crashed nuclear train in Odessa. However, Amid demonstrates his power of radioactivity by causing a glass of water in his hand to boil, showing that he can detonate a nuclear device all by himself.

Federal agents, following information Matt gained using his telepathy, break in. Amid is arrested – and he recognizes Matt. Tim Kring has explained that it was intended that the two knew each other from years before, when Amid stayed with Matt's family as a student.

Traces of the Amid Halebi character remain, largely through Ted Sprague (whose story also intertwines with Matt Parkman's), who displays a similar power and a tragic back-story.

INTRODUCTIONS

The idea behind the text crawl at the opening of the pilot was to create a bold, comic book-style vibe. The score used over it originally featured in the movie *Batman Begins*, and definitely helps set the dramatic tone. The narration by Mohinder that follows was added very late in the post-production process. The text reads as so:

In recent days, a seemingly random group of individuals has emerged with what can only be described as "special" abilities. Although unaware of it now, these individuals will not only save the world, but change it forever. This transformation from ordinary to extraordinary will not occur overnight. Every story has a beginning.
Volume One of their epic tale begins here ...

PAUL SYLAR?

Heroes villain Sylar doesn't even appear on screen in *Genesis* – in fact, Sylar actor Zachary Quinto hadn't even been cast at that point. However, in the unaired pilot, Mohinder is seen searching Chandra's New York apartment, where he comes across a cassette tape marked "Sylar". In the aired *Genesis,* this is the only mention of the villain. In the unaired pilot, playing the tape, Mohinder hears a conversation between his father and Paul Sylar (although the voices heard are not of the actors Erick Avari and Zachary Quinto – instead actors Ravi Kapoor and Miguel Ferrer fill the roles).

Mohinder discovers an entry in Chandra's notes showing the address of this Paul Sylar. He heads there, and discovers it decorated in grisly fashion with clippings about a series of brutal murders. He also finds a closet, its walls covered with disturbing scrawled phrases repeated over and over.

Back at his father's apartment, Mohinder runs into a figure wearing a dark trenchcoat and black hat. "Sylar!" he gasps, as the scene ends.

An early character set-up that was later abandoned in favor of the Gabriel Gray origin story, Tim Kring has said that NBC thought it was best that the main villain didn't appear until later on in the season, and he agreed.

IN HIS OWN IMAGE

The original idea for *Heroes* was to have multiple chapters in each episode, so the unaired pilot itself does not have a name (as we now know, actual episode titles would appear in their opening moments for the rest of the series). Chapter cards for the unaired pilot episode include:

Chapter One: *In His Own Image*
Chapter Two: *I'm Being Followed By A Moon Shadow*
Chapter Three: *Genesis or How I learned To Stop Worrying And Love The Bomb*
Multiple chapter cards were always in the original pilot script, but this was decided by the creative team to be too texty, and they were replaced in *Genesis* with the single chapter title card.

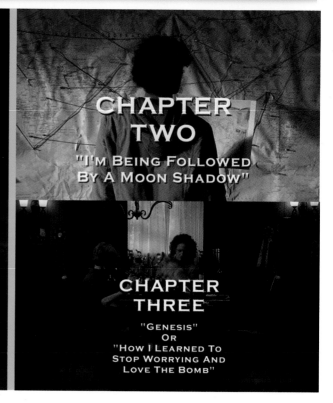

CHAPTER ONE
"IN HIS OWN IMAGE"

CHAPTER TWO
"I'M BEING FOLLOWED BY A MOON SHADOW"

CHAPTER THREE
"GENESIS" OR "HOW I LEARNED TO STOP WORRYING AND LOVE THE BOMB"

JEPH LOEB, COMIC GENIUS

As writer and co-executive producer, and someone who has been with the smash hit show from the very start, Jeph Loeb has plenty to share about *Heroes*. And that's before he even starts to talk about his illustrious career in movies, TV, and comics...

Jeph Loeb may be a creative genius, but to date, he hasn't used his talents to conquer the world, just Hollywood. Not only did he pen such cult 1980s features as *Teen Wolf* and *Commando*, but he also helped shape the earlier seasons of *Smallville* and then *Lost*. On top of all that, Loeb has become one of the comic book industry's most respected writers, most notably with *Batman: The Long Halloween*, the recent *Hulk* series, and the best-selling *Ultimates 3*. With those kinds of accomplishments, it is no wonder the producer/writer is one of the busiest guys around. Here, Loeb discusses his work on *Heroes* and his thoughts on the characters, plus he shares some hints about the show's much anticipated third chapter...

Before *Heroes*, you worked on *Lost*. How did this new series manage to steal you away?
JEPH LOEB: I have known [*Heroes* creator] Tim Kring for more years than either of us wants to admit! He called me before he'd written anything on the *Heroes* pilot episode and said he had an idea he wanted to talk to me about. Honestly, if you'd woken me up that day and said, "What do you think he's going to talk to you about?", I would have guessed he was retiring. *Crossing Jordan* was a huge hit and he and his wife are big wine fans, so they could have been opening up a winery in Napa Valley and wanted me to invest in it. I could not think of another thing. Instead, he came and had this idea about ordinary people developing extraordinary abilities. Because he doesn't read comics and he hasn't seen any of those movies, he just wanted me to be this sounding board to make sure he wasn't coming up with anything that had already been done. We started talking and he had the whole story mapped out.

Then, we made a date to get together and he came over to my office, and we went for a walk. We walked from Sherman Oaks to Universal City, which starts at 110th street, and we walked down the entire length of New York City. We talked for five hours and he had every single character and scene in mind.

What was the next step?
Tim finished the script, I read it, but I couldn't believe how he had translated what he had told me, and then secretly wondered to myself how he was going to film it. The next time I heard from him, it was getting towards the end of the season on *Lost*. He had more than a rough cut, but it certainly wasn't a finished cut of the pilot episode. He asked me to come over and took me to a tiny little office where we watched it on this huge screen. I was practically in the monitor, but it made for a very personal experience. I was so overwhelmed by it. I had no idea it was going to be so emotional, so character-driven, and really deliver on everything he wanted. It was 72 minutes long – the one shown at San Diego, which is now on the DVD.

He said, "What do you think?" and I said, "I start Monday morning." Tim was like, "I haven't even turned the pilot episode in. I don't know if I am going to get an order." I replied, "You are going to get an order and it is going to be a big smash hit and I want to be part of it."

"TIM KRING SHOWED ME A ROUGH CUT OF THE *HEROES* PILOT, AND SAID, 'WHAT DO YOU THINK?' AND I SAID, 'I START MONDAY MORNING.'"

Very quickly after that, he hired Aron Coleite, Joe Pokaski, Jesse Alexander, and then me. I never looked back.

Was there something specific in the pilot episode that required your superhero expertise?
Out of everything, the only thing I bumped on was [Kring] wanted a character that could lift up a truck and throw it. He could do that because he could control metal with his magnetic abilities. I said,

Future Peter, Niki, Adam, and Sylar – Loeb reveals that Tim Kring had *Heroes* mapped out from the start...

"Tim, that is Magneto!" He turned to me and said, "Is that a person or a power?" I thought it was so funny because I couldn't imagine anyone walking around going, "I have Magneto power!" I was like, "You have never seen an *X-Men* movie?" And he was like, "No."

Then, if you go look at episode 22, where Sylar tips over the armored car with Ted inside, that's where we finally placed it in. We figured how to do it telekinetically as opposed to magnetically.

Sounds like you are the go-to guy for super-hero information in the office.
Yeah, but it was actually a problem the first few days. [Producers] Aron and Joe would come by the office with comics and things for me to sign and I would go, "I can't. I work with you. It's like going to your sister and asking her to sign things." It was odd. I was flattered, but we got over it very quickly. Now they just make fun of me (*laughs*). Those guys are now writing comics and it's thrilling for me to see them break in. So I get to ask them for their autographs now!

Jesse Alexander was a big comic fan too. Then there was also [producers] Michael Green and Bryan Fuller. Big fans! Michael is writing *Superman/Batman* for DC now.

I think what is important is that I wasn't really hired because I was a comic-book person; the network didn't have any interest in that. They hired me because I was on *Smallville* and *Lost*. If I've used any of that comic-book world, it's been when we are breaking a story and I offer up an, "Umm no. You can't do that because it has been used before in issue so-and-so."

There was a real geek moment in the beginning where we talked about how a character was going to work. I said out loud, to my regret, "We're talking about Damage." Everyone turned around and said, "What are you talking about?" I was like, "He's kind of an obscure character in the DC Universe," and then the entire room went back to work. It was sort of like, "Thanks Grandpa." To this day, whenever I am rambling about some stupid idea, someone in the room

THE LIFE OF LOEB

TV/MOVIE CREDITS

Jeph Loeb's first writing credit was on the 1985 *Teen Wolf* movie, and he also wrote *Teen Wolf Too* in '87. He has also been a producer on the movies *Commando* ('85), *Burglar* ('87), and *Firestorm* ('98). Loeb was a consulting producer on *Smallville* from 2002 to 2005, and wrote four episodes. He was a supervising producer on *Lost* in 2006, and then joined the *Heroes* creative team as a co-executive producer and a writer of three episodes so far (*One Giant Leap*, *Unexpected*, and *Powerless*).

COMICS WORK

Jeph Loeb's first comic work was in 1991 on *Challengers of the Unknown* – his first collaboration with artist Tim Sale (who provides Isaac Mendez's drawings on *Heroes*). Since then, he has written a *Wolverine/Gambit* mini-series (1995, with Sale), before moving on to the acclaimed *Batman Halloween Specials* ('93), *Batman: The Long Halloween* ('97), and 2002's *Batman: Dark Victory* for DC Comics, followed by *Superman for all Seasons* ('98) and *Catwoman: When in Rome* (2005), all with Sale.

Since then, Loeb has worked with Sale on color-orientated limited series for Marvel: *Daredevil: Yellow* (2001), *Hulk: Gray* (2003), and he is currently producing a *Captain America: White* series (pictured above).

Recent writing gigs have included the ongoing *Superman/Batman* series for DC, the epic *Batman: Hush* storyline in 2003, and the *Fallen Son: Death of Captain America* series for Marvel. He is currently working on Marvel's *Ultimates 3*.

will inevitably go, "You know, we are talking about Damage."

In terms of storytelling, we carry a lot of balls in the air and there is a lot of interweaving. That's just part of the world I come from. I am much more interested in the characters and how they interact with each other than I am with whether the guy has laser eyes or not.

How has the casting influenced your take on the characters?
We had built Sylar up to be this gigantic monster and the easy way would have been some huge *Texas Chainsaw Massacre* kind of killer – and then we found Zach Quinto, who was slight and soft-spoken… It was a great marriage of casting and character.

A lot of the characters really came into their own once the actors were hired. In a lot of ways, *Five Years Gone* provided real inspiration for us. In more than any other episode, Milo [Ventimiglia] became a leading man and we saw a side of him we had never seen before, which allowed us to do more of what we did in season two.

Writer/producer Bryan Fuller was instrumental in shaping Claire's voice. In those developmental stages, was there a

character you nurtured more than another?
To be fair, Bryan absolutely spent a lot of time with Claire – so did a lot of other people in the room, including Tim who created her in the pilot. Similarly, I spent a lot of time on Niki, but so did the rest of the room. Mine were all the confusing parts (*laughter*). The scenes leading up to D.L.'s appearance were the things I took hold of. We really got to know Ali [Larter] very well in terms of her talent and we really stuck with that story. It is probably the character I wrote most during that season. There was some stuff with Matt that I really liked too, but that was later on.

In your second episode, *Unexpected*, Peter really shines as he learns from Claude, and then he faces off against H.R.G. and Isaac. How much fun was it showcasing those powers?
It was pretty amazing. You start off writing the script, but of course you then have to deliver on it and produce it. For example, I don't think anyone expected that

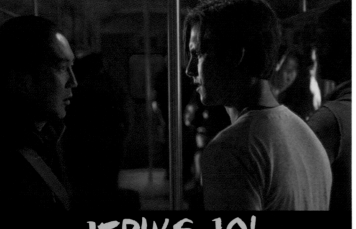

JEPH'S 10!
Jeph Loeb picks his top 10 most shocking moments of *Heroes'* first two seasons!

#10 – "In the pilot episode, you watch Peter fall off the building and you're waiting, waiting, waiting for him to fly… and it turned out to be Nathan who could fly. That was the first shocker I remember."

#9 – "The next shocker is probably everyone's favorite 'oh shit!' moment – it's when Claire said exactly that at the end of my first episode, *One Giant Leap*. You come across the autopsy table and find out Claire has been opened up. In the original script, the coroner had already started to take out her body organs! Claire reached over and took her heart and liver out of this bucket and started

stuffing them back in. That just became a little much for the network…"

#8 – "Sylar's killing of cheerleader Jackie – where her feet were dangling – was pretty brutal. It really brought home how cruel Sylar could be and what a monster he is."

#7 – "When we saw Future Hiro and he says, 'Peter Petrelli, I have a message for you.' That was pretty astonishing. It was the idea of a horrible future that was created by whatever was going to happen in our present. Given the fact that the show began with Hiro going into the future and seeing the atomic

Simone was going to walk in that door and get shot. But how could we make that work the best way to increase that shock? Greg Beeman and I worked a lot on *Smallville* and it was fun that the first episode he did was my first one too, which was episode three. We wound up working together on episode 16 and had developed a much greater shorthand between the two of us. I would just keep saying, "It's important the gun goes off," and then suddenly we cut to her standing there with a bullet wound in her. The audience has to make that connection. It is a very comic-book way of thinking about things. Comics are based upon panels that meet each other and you fill in the space of what happened between the drawings. I like to do that a lot in storytelling.

At the same time, in comics the sky is the limit when it comes to your imagination. Do you have to step back and scale it down for TV?
Sure, you have to be budget-conscious and that's something Jesse and I talk about a lot while the stories are breaking. The challenge we have on every episode of the show is if you're going to come over the hill and see an entire Japanese army, you need to see the army. But we are not making

Spider-Man for $250 million. We have a budget and a limited amount of time in order to shoot it with our effects, so we try and do it as effectively as possible.

> ## "IF SEASON ONE WAS ORDINARY PEOPLE DISCOVERING THEY HAD EXTRAORDINARY ABILITIES, SEASON TWO IS ABOUT HOW YOU GO BACK TO YOUR ORDINARY LIFE."

If season one set up the main characters and their situations, what were you hoping to accomplish with season two?
I always thought if season one was ordinary people discovering they had extraordinary abilities, now that they have an extraordinary ability, how do they go back to their ordinary life? How does Claire, who has traveled across the country and prevented the destruction of New York City, then go back to high school? How does Peter rediscover his power when he's lost his memory? Once Nathan realizes he has done something horrible and evil, how does he recapture what he had? That was really the challenge for the characters: what do you do the day after you save the world? What we found is once you touch that world, it's very hard to go back. The complications ensued from The Company, and some of the new characters we introduced enabled us to tell those stories.

How did the strike shake up the master-

Far left: Milo Ventimiglia really developed as a leading man; Left: Loeb discusses Adam's fate overleaf; This pic: Loeb reveals that he helped shape Niki's character

---

explosion, it just made sense that we could start to fool around with time travel and how much fun it could be. Then the idea that in the future, Hiro was a badass, there were a lot of conversations about whether he was going to have a sword or if it was too much over-the-top Samurai stuff, only to find out it is one of the most beloved parts of the show. The sword had its own whole history."

#6 – "When Peter died at the end of episode 11 on the steps of the

courthouse, that was a real breathtaking moment. Because we were in the first season and then we broke for Christmas break, I think a lot of the fans thought he was really dead. Good stuff."

#5 – "Another good shocker was when Peter is in a jail cell having a dream. He wakes up with Sylar next to him who says, 'You don't know anything about power.' Peter jumps away and realizes he is not really there. He was still in the dream. That was great."

#4 – "All of *Five Years Gone* was one big moment after another. You get to see our characters in the future and learn what would happen if the bomb did go off. The idea that Nathan turned out to be dead and replaced by Sylar was one of my favorite twists. It was writer Joe Pokaski's finest hour."

#3 – "The unedited version of Claire cutting off her toe in season two is so much more gruesome. I remember [producer/writer] Aron Coleite coming in saying, 'What if we do this?', and I thought it would be incredibly cool."

#2 – "In terms of cliffhangers, *Powerless* (episode 11, season two) demonstrates what our show does best. Nathan being shot and Sylar coming back are both 'Holy shit – did they just do that?' moments. I thought it was particularly 'us' when Sylar TK'd the tin can, indicating his powers were back, and we made it a spinach can. It was an inside joke you either get or you don't."

#1 – "But my favorite of favorites? Going back to episode 23, *How to Stop an Exploding Man*, when Molly Walker says she can find anyone except for one person, and when they ask her why, she says, 'When I look at him, he can see me.' She played it brilliantly for such a young actress and it was an amazing 'boo moment'."

plan for those final episodes in season two?
It didn't in a major way. It did in some of the storylines, but the Niki, Sylar, and Suresh storylines were completely untouched. It was always supposed to be the end of the volume, but not the end of the season. Tim, Jesse, and I had breakfast the morning before the weekend we went on strike. We came up with a way to end the Nathan story, which we were going to do later that year. We took it to the network that morning, and they green-lit it. I hammered out some scenes and we shot all weekend, right up to the deadline. It was wild. We used to joke that if we took over *24*, we would change the title to *'9'*. There were some other things going on in the Texas story and with the conflict Nathan was having over what to do. Once we knew the strike was coming, we realized it was better to accelerate that. Nathan was always going to decide to go in front of the camera and tell everyone they had powers, but that was going to happen later in the season. That changed the scenes that came before it.

Adam proved to be a worthy new adversary for our Heroes too.
I give David Anders a lot of credit. He played the part with such loathsome glee. It's something we do well on the show – we took your expectations of who this man was and we twisted it. We talked about him being the greatest warrior of all time and he turns out to be a drunkard and a lout, and because of what Hiro did, he becomes a villain. Then with the twist that he was Adam, we just couldn't get there soon enough. We spent all this time with him in Japan and then the idea he outlived them all and wanted to destroy the world because of what happened made it a compelling place to go.

Burying Adam was an ingenious and haunting way to take care of him…
At one point, we had talked about whether Hiro would take him to the bottom of the ocean and I just couldn't get my head around what that would look like. I was afraid it would look like a fish tank. Instead, we had spent so much time in cemeteries that it felt it was so much more horrible to bury him alive. Interestingly enough, the way it was written and shot was that you came across the cemetery and went down into the earth until you find Adam. It was Beeman in the editing room who offered up what might be more interesting – to start with him screaming, not knowing where he is, and then pulling up until you reveal he is in a cemetery. That was more powerful. And again, that is the joy of the show. Anybody who has a good idea gets to be heard. It makes for a great work environment and a better show.

"SUPPOSE THAT FIVE SYLARS DECIDE TO GO AFTER OUR GUYS IN SEASON THREE… ARE OUR GUYS PREPARED FOR THAT?"

At this point, what ideas are brewing for chapter three?
I can't reveal what is going to go on, but think about the basic concept of ordinary people waking up to extraordinary abilities, and now add the layer of an ordinary person waking up… except they're evil and have a power – *then* what happens? Suppose it wasn't Sylar, but five Sylars, and they decide to go after our guys? Are our guys prepared for that? When you think about if they were attacked aggressively… well, a lot of their powers are very passive…

Lastly, what was it like going on the *Heroes* 2007 tour?
It was awesomely amazing. I've done a lot of comic book conventions, so I certainly know what it's like to hang out with 50 or 100 people cheering you on. What made this unique was it was incredibly intimate. There was a lot of smaller gatherings, even though when we were in New York, there were 10,000 people who came out for the DVD thing at The Rockefeller Center.

I had this wonderful geek moment where [*Today* presenter] Al Roker was meeting Zach and Dania [Ramirez] and suddenly he turns and goes, "Oh my God! You are Jeph Loeb!" And I went, "Oh my God! You are Al Roker!" I thought he was messing around with me, but he was like "No, no! I have read *Long Halloween*! I've read…" I was like, "Al! You are a geek!" and he said, "I was a geek a long time ago!" Sometimes stuff like that happens that's completely unexpected. Just being able to thank our fans was a real gift.

THE HOUR

HIRO NAKAMURA HAS TELEPORTED ACROSS THE
WORLD, TRAVELED BACK TO 17TH CENTURY JAPAN, AND
GOTTEN HIMSELF INTO ALL SORTS OF ADVENTURES, AND
IT'S FAIR TO SAY HE'S HAVING THE TIME OF HIS LIFE. THE
SAME CAN BE SAID FOR MASI OKA, THE LIVELY ACTOR
WHO PORTRAYS HIM.
MASI DISCUSSES ALL THINGS *HEROES* AND HIRO…

TSALE
2006

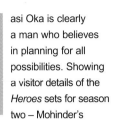

Masi Oka is clearly a man who believes in planning for all possibilities. Showing a visitor details of the *Heroes* sets for season two – Mohinder's apartment (sans Mohinder the lizard, who's not working today), the Irish pub where Peter's staying, and the new residence of the Bennet (or "Butler") family – Oka not only has the patter but the moves down, indicating which way to follow him by bending his elbows backward, just like a professional tour leader. Asked about his proficiency, Oka says with a grin, "If the acting doesn't work out, I can get a job at NBC/Universal Studios as a tour guide!"

This doesn't seem like it's going to be necessary. Oka's portrayal of *Heroes*' teleporting, time-bending optimist Hiro Nakamura made him arguably the biggest break-out TV star of the 2006-2007 season, earning him rave reviews, Emmy and Golden Globe nominations, and a whole legion of fans.

Born in Tokyo, Japan, Masiyori Oka moved with his family to the United States when he was six, resulting in his fluency in both Japanese and English. He attended Brown University, then was hired by Industrial Light & Magic as a computer special effects artist. Oka has played guest roles on a variety of TV series and has appeared in feature films including *Austin Powers in Goldmember*, *Balls of Fury*, *Get Smart* with Steve Carell, and *Quebec*.

What did you think of Hiro's character when you first read the pilot script?
MASI OKA: I thought it was phenomenal, because it wasn't one-note. Tim Kring created an amazing, beautiful world, with such rich characters. I'm just very fortunate to have Tim entrust me with the character.

Did you have to do any research in order to play Hiro?
I didn't need to do too much, because there were a lot of things I could relate to. I understand the culture, having grown up with the Japanese media a lot – I watch Japanese television and read Japanese magazines and comics, as well as American media. So it allowed me to understand Hiro's culture, his work and where he's coming from. So the research was probably more about the American comics I'm not too familiar with – I know the big ones, of course, but there's a wonderful sub-genre of comics in America; the beautiful art that Tim Sale [who does the paintings of Isaac, Sylar, and Peter on the show] is doing. But other than that, in terms of who Hiro is, I'm quite familiar with the character!

Do you have to psych yourself up to reach Hiro's level of energy?
I tend to be very passionate and energetic as well. Luckily, being on set and working with such an amazing crew and cast is always exciting, so it definitely carries me through. A lot of it is definitely self-generating enthusiasm, so, as I said, I do carry a piece of Hiro with me and I feel like I don't have to try that hard to be as enthusiastic as Hiro – it's definitely an exaggerated version of me.

Is there anything you do differently as an actor in *Heroes* that you don't do in non-fantasy projects?
I might heighten a little bit of my movement and my facial reactions, just because there's

"I DO CARRY A PIECE OF HIRO WITH ME AND I FEEL LIKE I DON'T HAVE TO TRY THAT HARD TO BE AS ENTHUSIASTIC WITH HIRO. HE'S DEFINITELY AN EXAGGERATED VERSION OF ME."

a language barrier. The whole idea is, this is a realistic show. It's about ordinary people getting extraordinary abilities, and we want everyone to feel it's real and not something campy. Because of the language barrier, I do feel like I dial it up a little bit, because I need to communicate through my body and my expression more so than through my words, but it's not a genre thing.

When you began your acting career, did you want to work in science fiction?
I pretty much came into acting wanting to do comedic roles, because I know how hard it is for Asian actors in the US, and comedy is

something that I feel usually transcends any – quote-unquote – racial barriers or perceptions that one might have. So that's what I focused on. Even in *Heroes*, I get to play a non-conformist computer anime enthusiast. He is the only one [at the outset] who enjoys having a power, and he's comedic relief for this very dramatic and real and dark show.

What was your first acting job in L.A.?

My first TV job in Los Angeles was for a pilot called *Straight White Male*. It was for the FX Channel, and it didn't get picked up, but I recall it pretty well, because getting that job allowed me to continue working for ILM in a telecommuting capacity while pursuing acting down in Los Angeles.

Are you still working for ILM?
I'm still on their payroll. I work a day out of the week. Unfortunately, I can't really say I'm developing anything new, because that was my specialty there, but I'm more like a consultant, reading, advising – I love Industrial Light & Magic. They're so patient

with my acting career as well – they've given me opportunities I would never [otherwise] have, so I always want to be loyal to them.

Do you talk to the *Heroes* special effects team about their work on the show?
[Working as an effects artist], I remember spending months and months to get 200 [CGI] frames [completed]. Our effects folks are doing a bang-up job. It's really cool to be able to talk about that on the set and have that kind of camaraderie there. As a special effects person, it's neat to be on the other side. When I'm in front of that green screen, I'm like, "Oh, I've got to make sure the hair

Future Hiro?
There's definitely a lot of challenge in it. It's actually a gift that the writers gave me – to throw this Future Hiro in when we first saw him in episode four [*Collision*] on the Subway. When you play a character that's so different, you need a lot of back-story and preparation. The writers gave me just enough information to know what that character needed to go through, and I was just so grateful that they trusted me to give me this gift. It was definitely fun to play it, although I have to say Future Hiro in episode 20 [*Five Years*

> "WHEN I'M PLAYING FUTURE HIRO, I'M DEFINITELY IN THAT DARK MODE AND I PUT MYSELF IN THAT MENTALITY. IT'S A LOT MORE INTENSE."

strands aren't out there, because that's going to be hard to matte out." In season one's episode 21 [*The Hard Part*], when I was acting against myself as Future Hiro, they explained to me, "Okay, we're going to comp you here and here, and we're going to do four layers [of effects]." And that makes total sense to me. We have a total respect and understanding of each other. You have to understand how the elements work and how to layer all the comps.

I love fantasy and I love science and I love art. It's what I studied at college, theatre arts and computer science, plus math. The idea of being able to use both sides of the brain is fascinating to me. I feel society "typecasts" you sometimes to use only one side, and a human being has so much more potential, and that's why I want to do both. Luckily, I have the opportunity to utilize both in harmony.

Can you talk about the differences between playing "our" Hiro and badass

MASI OKA
SELECTED CREDITS

TV

Heroes – Hiro Nakamura *(2006-)*
Robot Chicken – Japanese Fred Rogers (2007)
The Sarah Silverman Program – Clerk (2007)
Joey – Arthur (2006)
Without a Trace – Wei Fan (2006)
Reba – IRS Agent Phung (2006)
Scrubs (2002-2004) – Franklyn
Sabrina the Teenage Witch (2002) – Male Council Member
Gilmore Girls (2001) – Philosophy Student
Dharma & Greg (2001) – Nien-Jen

MOVIES

Get Smart (2008) – Bruce
Balls of Fury (2007) – Jeff, Bathroom Attendant
House of the Dead 2 (2005) – Stanley Tong
Along Came Polly (2004) – Wonsuk

Legally Blonde 2: Red, White & Blonde (2003) – Congressional Intern
Austin Powers in Goldmember (2002) – Japanese Pedestrian

SPECIAL EFFECTS WORK
Masi Oka has worked on the following movies...
Pirates of the Carribean: Dead Man's Chest (2006)
War of the Worlds (2005)
Star Wars Episode III: Revenge of the Sith (2005)
Terminator 3: Rise of the Machines (2003)
Hulk (2003)
Dreamcatcher (2003)
Star Wars Episode II: Attack of the Clones (2002)
The Perfect Storm (2000)
Star Wars Episode I: The Phantom Menace (1999)
Mighty Joe Young (1998)

HIRO LINGO

Learn how to speak some key Hiro phrases in Japanese!

"I am special. I am a hero!"
"Ore wa tokubetsu dayo. Ore wa hiiroo nano sa!"
"おれは特別だよ。おれはヒーローなのさ！"

"Where is my sword?"
"Katana wa doko da?"
"刀はどこだ？"

"I love Charlie Andrews…"
"Chaarii Andoriyuuzu ga daisuki nanda."
"チャーリー・アンドリューズが大好きなんだ。"

"Mr. Isaac is a great artist!"
"Aizakku-san wa subarashii aatisuto nanda."
"アイザックさんは素晴らしいアーティストなんだ。"

"My hero is Takezo Kensei."
"Ore no hiiroo wa Kensei Takezo da."
"おれのヒーローは剣聖 武蔵だ。"

"Oh no, I'm in trouble again!"
"Yabai! Mata pinchi!"
"やばい！またピンチ！"

Gone], when he went five years into the future, was kind of a pain to work with, because he'd never show up on set... He'd say, "Here, use a blue screen instead of me." He wouldn't even be there for our lines – he'd record his dialogue and then have it played back. So I've never actually met Future Hiro in person. I'm sure he's a nice guy, but I don't know – I guess after five years, all that fame goes to his head.

I love them both. Present Hiro's a lot more fun for me because, you know, you get to have fun. When I'm doing Future Hiro, I'm definitely in that dark mode and I put myself in that mentality, so it's a little bit more difficult, it's a lot more intense, but they're both great characters.

How do you feel about your Emmy nomination?
A big thank-you to Tim [Kring]! I'm definitely floored and humbled [by the Outstanding Supporting Actor nomination]. Personally, it's an honor to be able to work hard, to be sure I portray

WORKING WITH A HERO'S HERO

While Hiro Nakamura is working with his childhood legend Takezo Kensei, actor Masi Oka has gotten to act with one of his real-life cultural heroes, George Takei, who plays Hiro's stern father, Kaito Nakamura.

"He's not only a generous actor, but a generous person," Oka enthuses. "He's an icon in every aspect of Asian-American TV and cinema. You learn so much from him. And if you were to ask George, he would say (*does deep-voiced impression of Takei*), 'Well, I found working with Masi to be quite an experience. He's quite a young and talented individual. And it's nice to see the sci-fi generation torch get passed from the older to the younger, and the legacy being kept alive. Ha, ha, ha!'"

The sword-fighting lesson between Oka and Takei was a highlight, Oka adds. "We didn't get to rehearse that much, because of George's schedule and my schedule, but when we did it, it was great. And George is so in shape! He's almost 70, I believe. We said, 'Okay, George, we'll take it very slow, and if worse comes to the worst, we've got a stunt double.' George is fantastic. It was a 12-step choreography, he learned it all and he memorized everything. We were able to use a lot of the cuts. It was definitely cool to do."

the character in the best way possible that enables him to be approachable and kind of the average everyman that viewers can imagine themselves being. Just to be part of this ensemble is a gift, and to have an Emmy nomination is a cherry on top.

Did you expect *Heroes*' Emmy nomination for Best Drama Series?
I'm definitely proud of our nomination [for Best Drama Series]. I was pretty confident the show would get nominated, actually. I was hanging out with Zachary Quinto that night, and we were going to stay up and watch the announcement, so we could share the glory together. Unfortunately, we fell asleep, but we had a very nice wake-up call. To have our Emmy nomination reflects the hard work that we've all put in on the show, because that's a tribute to what everyone has done. It's a culmination of all the hard work that the writers, the crew, the cast, all put in. It's nice to have that affirmation – that not only is it a big hit with the audience, but it's also accepted in the critical minds. I think it's a validation of

the show as a quality show.

How was the *Heroes* panel at Comic-Con 2007?
It was kind of like winning the Super Bowl and going back to your home city. Comic-Con is where [the fan support for *Heroes*] started, and it was just a great celebration of the phenomenon we've all created together – the fans, the writers, the cast. I wore the "Hayden Is My Hero" T-shirt. I even got a chance to walk the [convention] floor and interact with some of the fans.

There's so much love and passion for our show, and it was phenomenal just to be a part of that celebration.

Do you feel that Hiro Nakamura gives some hope to geeks everywhere?
Oh, yeah. If I can represent the geeks, I'm very fortunate to be able to do that. For me, the notion of a geek is someone who's passionate about something, whether it's computers, ant-farms or musicals, storytelling, or paperweights – anything you're passionate about! And that's what makes us human. It defines us as individuals. It gives us our uniqueness.

And I think it's more human, it's more commendable to be a geek and be passionate about something than be apathetic about everything.

Were you a comic book fan?
I was definitely a genre fan growing up. I was a *Star Wars* fan. I didn't grow up on American comics, either – I saw the movies that portrayed them – but I grew up reading Japanese manga comics, so most of my comic book heroes come from the Japanese manga world. Tezuka Osamu was fantastic. These days, I'm a big fan of Urasawa Naoki, who's actually doing an homage to Tezuka Osamu. He currently has a series called *Pluto*, which is loosely based on *Atomic Boy*. And growing up, I was a big fan of the kid stuff, the Fujiko Fujios and the Toriyama Akiras, all those fantastic authors and comic book artists. Manga is a part of our culture. I grew up with it in

Japan, and I'm fortunate enough to keep in touch with that world in America with imported comic books.

What are you passionate about?
I'm enjoying life right now. I get to meet so many great people. I guess that's what I'm really passionate about these days – just to be able to work on a great show, first of all. Then from there, I also get to meet great people, whether it's my cast, the writers, just going down the street, the fans. It's just really cool. Experiencing life right now is what I'm passionate about.

Do the *Heroes* plot twists still surprise you?
Oh, gosh. Every week's always a surprise. All of the actors – we're all big fans of the show. We just can't wait to read the scripts, even more now in season two. You think, "Oh, how can they top that…?" The writers always find a way to surprise us and put smiles on everyone's faces. It puts us on the edge of our seats, just wanting to know what happens next. I'm going to leave you wanting to know what happens next.

"HIRO IS THE ONLY ONE [AT THE OUTSET] WHO ENJOYS HAVING A POWER, AND HE'S COMEDIC RELIEF FOR THIS VERY DRAMATIC AND REAL AND DARK SHOW."

THE POWERS THAT BE

A look at HIRO NAKAMURA'S abilities

What is the power? How does it work?

Hiro seems, at first glance, to have two special abilities. One is the power to slow or stop time, as he does when he freezes the entire street to save a little girl from getting run over by a truck. The other is the power to travel instantaneously through time and space, as he does when he teleports to New York a few weeks in the future (an unrealized future, thanks to him). In fact, these are two aspects of the same gift: Hiro has the ability to move freely through time and space, and to move at different speeds relative to time's normal flow, which confines the rest of us. Hiro doesn't actually make time stop, he just steps outside of its current. While a nanosecond passes for those around him, Hiro might have the equivalent of minutes or hours to steal a museum display, disarm a band of nasty warriors, or stop an old friend from starting a global pandemic.

When did it first manifest?

Hiro tests his powers in tiny ways at first. He moves his desk clock's second-hand backwards for one second; teleports himself into the ladies' restroom of a karaoke bar; perhaps even makes the subway 14 seconds late. Then, spurred on by his desire for greatness, and by Ando's skepticism, he decides to try something big. Staring at a subway travel poster of New York, he concentrates hard. Behind him the digital clock speeds up to a blur and… "Yatta! Hello, New York!" He's standing in Times Square.

I did it!

"HIRO, THERE ARE 12 AND A HALF MILLION PEOPLE IN THIS CITY. NOT ONE OF THEM CAN BEND SPACE AND TIME. WHY DO YOU WANT TO BE DIFFERENT?"

"WHY DO YOU WANT TO BE THE SAME?"

ANDO AND HIRO, *GENESIS*

Maximum power

Hiro has a number of surprising moments as his powers develop. His teleportation of himself and Ando into the future is the first revelation that he can take people with him through both time and space. The biggest surprise, though, and the biggest jump, is the emergency teleport he makes to avoid slamming into a building in Kirby Plaza. Without effort, and certainly without intention, he ends up on the other side of the world, and 400 years in the past.

Maximum potential

Hiro's teleportation of Ando may only be the start of his ability to take others with him through time and space. When Future Hiro wants to talk to Peter privately, he stops time for everyone in the subway car, but brings Peter into his own temporal frame. As Hiro's control of his power grows, he may have the potential to teleport others and to move time around them, without even touching them, or even without going along himself. He may eventually learn to remotely teleport anyone or anything he wishes, to any time or place he can target. Perhaps the next time Hiro is faced with a nuclear holocaust, he'll have the ability to teleport an entire city out of its path. Or perhaps he will just stand at a safe distance and teleport the nuke into space, without even scrunching up his face.

Hiro's ability to move through time seems to come even more naturally to him than teleportation. His first attempts at big teleportation jumps nearly always end up carrying him through time as well as space – eight weeks, five years, 400 years. If he can do this so easily that it comes by accident, his time travel abilities could be virtually unlimited.

His manipulation of time, and his reaction time, is so precise that it can be measured in nano-seconds. He stops Hope's bullets in the interval between the firing of the gun, and the time it takes bullets to travel a few feet – to normal human perception, no interval at all. With practice, Hiro could learn to respond to events around him, before anyone else can even perceive that something has happened.

What Hiro does to Hope's bullets holds the greatest potential of all: he seems to make them move backwards in time, actually *unfiring* the gun. The power of rewinding time moment by moment could have extraordinary consequences – both good and bad.

Biggest act of heroism

In rescuing Yaeko, Hiro falls in love with her. But because he believes she is destined to win the heart of Takezo Kensei, he keeps his love a secret. Even when she unmasks him, he resists his love for her. And finally, he gives her up for good to return to his own time. Talk about ripping out your own heart!

TAKEZO KENSEI

Hiro was weaned on the legends of Takezo Kensei. When he meets the real Kensei, he learns that reality and legend don't always match up. How much of the legend is Hiro, and how much is the Englishman we later know as Adam Monroe?

Kensei, "Sword Saint"
In legend, the title was given to Takezo after he learned from a dragon to master a special sword. In reality, Adam adopted this grandiose name to intimidate his enemies.

"Saving the village of Otsu"
No such luck. Though the Swordsmith paid Takezo to defend the village, Hiro's unexpected arrival messes up his planned ambush. Otsu is burned and the Swordsmith is captured by White Beard.

"The Battle of Twelve Swords and Rescue of the Swordsmith's Daughter"
Hiro, disguised in Takezo's armor, uses his powers to strip the warriors of their swords and bows, and rescues Yaeko from them.

"Fall in Love with the Swordsmith's Daughter"
Both men do so, and Yaeko loves Takezo, until she discovers that the man who first rescued her was in fact Hiro, not Takezo.

"The Fire Scroll and the 90 Angry Ronins"
Hiro teleports Takezo to the steps of the temple and leaves him there to face the Ronins, assuming, correctly, that his regenerative powers will help him defeat them and capture the scroll.

"Kill the Black Bear of Sakashita; Climb the Frozen Waterfall, Find the Single Crimson Peony."
Hiro writes to Ando that he helped Takezo accomplish each of these "trials", all pieces of a plan to rescue Yaeko's father, the Swordsmith.

"Defeat White Beard and save Japan"
Takezo is on-board with the plan to blow up White Beard's arsenal of guns, until he sees Hiro and Yaeko kissing. Betrayed, he hands them over to White Beard. So Hiro and Yaeko rescue themselves and carry out the plan together, leaving Takezo presumed dead.

"Tear out his heart for love of the Princess"
Hiro does this metaphorically, when he leaves Yaeko to return to his own time. But one could say that Takezo does it too, as he metaphorically tears out his heroic heart in jealousy and swears to be Hiro's enemy forever.

Though Hiro believes that his arrival in the past has damaged history and threatened the Legend of Kensei, the reverse is more likely the truth. Takezo was a mercenary and a trickster before Hiro arrived, one who never would have become a hero on his own. Without Hiro, the Swordsmith and Yaeko would have been executed, and White Beard would have used his arsenal of forbidden firearms to conquer Japan and end the samurai tradition. When Hiro's quest in the past is finished, Yaeko swears to remember and honor him by telling the story of Takezo Kensei – Hiro's story – to everyone. By going back into the past, however accidentally, Hiro actually created the legend he was raised on. His ideal of heroism comes from his own actions trying to fulfill that ideal. It's a classic temporal paradox.

Best use of powers

Once Hiro learns of the destruction of New York, nearly everything he does with his powers is heroic, because he is trying to save the world, and some of the most important people in it: Claire, Charlie, Ando, his father. Perhaps his finest moment is when he returns to the moment of his father's murder, intending to prevent it. But when he takes Kaito into the past, he accepts his father's wisdom that he must not use his powers to play God. In doing so, he gives Kaito a son's greatest gift: the knowledge that he has truly learned to honor his father's lessons.

Worst use of powers

Though Hiro believes a Hero should never use his powers for personal gain, stopping time to cheat a little in a Las Vegas poker game is a relatively minor sin. The way Hiro stops his one-time friend, Adam, is on a different level. There's no question that Adam needs to be stopped before he can find another way to destroy the world. But surely Hiro could have found a safe and humane way to do it, especially if he had consulted with his friends and allies. Several others, including Peter and Claire, know how to kill a man with the power to regenerate indefinitely. Instead Hiro takes justice into his own hands and leaves Adam buried alive in a Japanese graveyard – a fate far worse than death for a man who can't die. Is this justice? Or is it revenge for his father's murder? And what will happen if Adam finds a way to escape his living tomb?

Biggest dangers

When Hiro fails to save Charlie, he loses his powers. This is a potential danger for all Heroes. The mind is so important in the use of their powers, that a Hero who loses faith in himself may be unable to call on his abilities when he has to, to save others or himself.

Unanswered questions

Does Hiro actually have the power to make other objects, like Hope's bullets, and people move backward along their own path in time? And if so, how does this work, and how is it related to his other powers?

Hiro's time-traveling brings up the most common of temporal paradoxes. He made three attempts to change the past: he tried to save Charlie; he tried to stop the destruction of New York by saving the cheerleader; and he tried to make Kensei into the hero of Japanese legend. He succeeded completely only in saving New York, and failed to save Charlie, but his actions in medieval Japan made the legend of Takezo Kensei a reality in spite of Takezo's failures. How much can a time-traveling Hero actually change the past that he remembers, and how much does it exist as he knows it, because he has already gone back to fix it?

Looking badass

Our Hiro is the perfect nice-guy geek, with his big glasses, messy hair, and permanent smile. What a shock, then, to see a very different Hiro coming toward Peter on the subway. This Hiro, with his tiny beard and sleek Samurai ponytail, speaks perfect English, moves with intense focus and determination, and, coolest of all, wears a sword. It's our first glimpse of Future Hiro, who so embodies the full meaning of badass, that when the two Hiros come face to face in the future, our Hiro tells Ando that Future Hiro scares him!

How the powers change his life

Hiro is one of the few Heroes to welcome his new life. While others with special abilities fear that they are becoming freaks, Hiro is delighted to discover that at last, he's more than a cubicle drone. He experiments with his powers, and expounds to Ando the obligations of a Hero. Once Hiro has seen the future and understands what is at stake, he begins to become, in truth, the Hero that has always been hidden within the office worker. Guided by the notions of heroism he learned from his father's bedtime stories, Hiro dedicates himself to saving first the future, then the past. He undertakes whatever he must to carry out his missions, and never cares how crazy he looks to those around him. He starts by merely risking his job and his father's wrath, and goes on traveling in time, facing unthinkable enemies, and even accepting the loss of his father and the two women he loves.

Best of all, his quest brings him to a new and closer bond with his father. Kaito recognizes the Hero in his son, the Hero he always hoped to raise, and helps Hiro to fulfill his destiny.

SINS OF THE FATHER

AS *STAR TREK*'S SULU, GEORGE TAKEI PORTRAYED A PLAYFUL, LIKEABLE CHARACTER – BUT HIS LATEST ROLE HAS BEEN SOMEWHAT DIFFERENT. PLAYING HIRO NAKAMURA'S FATHER, KAITO, TAKEI HAS TAKEN ON A STERN, INTIMIDATING PERSONA WHOSE DEADLY SECRETS ULTIMATELY RESULT IN HIS MURDER. THE TV LEGEND GIVES HIS TAKE ON EVENTS...

George Takei looks perfectly at home in the elegance of an up-market hotel in London's Covent Garden. Chatting about the *Star Trek* remastered DVDs and sipping tea, he answers every question with a twinkle in his eye, being careful not to give too much away when the topic turns to *Heroes*. At the time we talk initially, Kaito Nakamura's surprise reappearance in season two's ninth episode, *Cautionary Tales*, had yet to air, but we caught up with him at the start of the new year in 2008 to bring everything up to date…

Takei has been a legend in science fiction circles for four decades, since *Star Trek* started airing in 1966. His portrayal of Hikaru Sulu, the helmsman of the original *Starship Enterprise* who's secretly a swashbuckler at heart, won him fans around the world. As a prominent member of the gay and Japanese-American communities, Takei has campaigned on numerous political issues, and he currently enjoys a role as sidekick to Howard Stern on the shock jock's radio show.

As a child growing up in Los Angeles, Takei was a big comic book fan. "I had a fantastic collection of Superman and Batman comic books that I treasured, but when I went off to college at U.C. Berkeley, my mother decided to clean everything out," he reminisces. "And you know what she cleaned out? She said, 'George is off to college now, so he's no longer going to need these old comic books.' So she had the man who comes by to collect old newspapers take them away. When I came back and discovered they were missing, I was devastated – but that's what happens with so many young comic book collectors. You go away and your parents don't share the same passion that you have. To them, it's just old newspaper – a fire-trap!"

With a huge grin on his face, he admits that he's having a great time working on *Heroes*, even though it wasn't a show that he watched when it first aired. However, his public presence on the internet means that fans have moderately easy access to Takei. "My computer became peppered with emails from *Star Trek* fans telling me that there was a Japanese character who is a *Star Trek* fan on this new TV series called *Heroes*," he recalls. "I thought I should check this out, so I started watching it and got hooked. It's a very addictive show with the cliff-hangers and so forth.

"I was enjoying the show innocently until my agent called and said that the people at *Heroes* wanted me on the show. The Hiro character is Japanese and has a Japanese-speaking friend, so I said,

'That'll be fun.' He said, 'They want you to play his father.' I said, 'Oh, that's going to be even more fun!' and then he said, 'They want you to audition for that part.'"

That came as something of a surprise to the veteran actor, who has more than 130 credits on different shows to his name. "Generally when they want me for a part, they know what I can do, so they don't audition me," he points out. "But they wanted to audition me. I said, 'Sure, I'll do it.' I don't have any ego problems there."

The second surprise came when the material for the audition was emailed to Takei. "It was all in English," he recalls. "I called my agent and said I thought he would be speaking Japanese. He said that they wanted me to translate it. I thought, 'Oh my!'"

"*Heroes* is a very addictive show. I was enjoying the show innocently and then my agent called and said that the people at *Heroes* wanted me..."

Takei went ahead and prepared the translation. "I went and met a whole battery of people. It was like a small theatre. There were about two dozen people in that room. It was quite intimidating. And there wasn't a single Asian face there. The person I read with was a blonde Caucasian girl. I did the scene and they liked what I did. Afterwards I asked the woman – who had a terrible accent, incidentally – where she learned her accent, and she said she lived in Japan for a few months but she had studied here in the US.

"I came back thinking it was a fascinating experience. I had never used my Japanese in any of my work before, and certainly I've never worked in Japan in a film. I've done *Star Trek* conventions there but that audition was the first time I've professionally used my Japanese, so that was fun. They called back and said I had the part."

Takei has spoken Japanese fluently since he was a child. "My parents sent me to Japanese language school, which any child hates. All the other kids are off playing on a Saturday so why did I have to go to school another day? But the reward was summer school in Tokyo, so I did study hard so I could be prepared for my summers there.

"This was the first time I'd acted in Japanese, and it was challenging. Despite the fact that I speak Japanese, it's easier to memorize in English. For the translation, there were some words that I had to look up in the dictionary like 'ancestral legacy.' As a matter of fact, *Heroes* has increased my vocabulary because I have had to look up words and they do have a Japanese consultant on the set. She provides a wonderful opportunity to practice – I chat with her on the set in Japanese just to keep my language skills up!"

Takei wasn't given much to go on when he received the first script in which Kaito Nakamura appeared. "He didn't have a single word to utter," he laughs. In *The Fix*, all we see of Hiro's father is him stepping out of a very expensive vehicle.

"I knew that he was a very powerful businessman, a powerful industrialist, one of the richest men in the world." Takei adds. "The producers told me that the car that they provided me with cost something like $350,000. It was a really impressive vehicle. And I knew that Kaito was very concerned about this weirdo son that he has. In the good Japanese tradition, he wanted his son to follow in his footsteps.

"The second script [*Distractions*] confirmed that, and certainly gave me more to sink my teeth into. I found Kaito to be a fascinating character. I thought he was primarily a powerful father, profoundly concerned and worried about his son and the legacy that he was going to leave behind."

However, as the scripts for the latter part of the first season arrived, Takei realized that he had "been playing that role wrong. The producers don't inform you fully of the character – they like to keep the actors in ignorance because we do interviews, and journalists are very clever at ferreting out or reading in between what we say! My loins are girded! To protect their storylines, they do keep the actors in the dark. We don't know what's going to happen until we get the script."

Takei learned that his past history on *Star Trek* contributed to one of Kaito's skills. In the *Trek* episode *The Naked Time*, Sulu is

George Takei Selected Credits

TV

Heroes – Kaito Nakamura (2007)
Kim Possible – Sensei (2003-2007)
Star Trek: New Voyages – Sulu (2007)
Malcolm in the Middle – As himself (2006)
Scrubs – Priest (2004)
The Simpsons – Akira (1991, 1999, 2001)
Murder, She Wrote – Bert Tanaka (1987)
General Hospital – Diem (1963)
The Six Million Dollar Man – Chin Lang (1974)
Star Trek – Sulu (1966-1969)
Mission Impossible – Roger Lee (1966)
Hawaiian Eye – Hiroshi Kawagani (1960-1961)

MOVIES

The Great Buck Howard – As himself (2008)
The Eavesdropper – Dr. Hsiesh (2004)
Who Gets the House? – Elliott (1999)
Mulan – First Ancestor (1998)
Star Trek VI: The Undiscovered Country – Sulu (1991)
Star Trek V: The Final Frontier – Sulu (1989)
Return from the River Kwai – Lt. Tanaka (1989)
Star Trek IV: The Voyage Home – Sulu (1986)
Star Trek III: The Search for Spock – Sulu (1984)
Star Trek: The Wrath of Khan – Sulu (1982)
Star Trek: The Motion Picture – Sulu (1979)
Which Way to the Front? – Yamashita (1970)
Red Line 7000 – Kato (1965)

revealed to be an expert swordsman. "The writers visit the set occasionally, and we get a chance to casually chit-chat with them. I discovered that the teaching of the sword to my son in *Landslide* came about because one of the writers on the team was a *Star Trek* fan. He remembered *The Naked Time* and thought, 'Why don't we work a sword-fighting sequence into the character of Kaito Nakamura?' *Star Trek* is always intertwined somewhere in my life."

The actor agrees that as the season progressed, the character of Kaito became more three-dimensional. He never softened his attitudes towards work and his legacy, but we saw other sides to him. "He still is a very stern, determined man," says Takei. "He has goals to accomplish and he will accomplish them. He's concerned because his son doesn't appear to have that – until he makes a few more discoveries. For example, we go back and forth in time, and you see him as a young father reading to his son. I thought that that was all that it was – I didn't know that the legend of Takezo Kensei, that I was reading to Hiro, was going to be another subplot in the saga of *Heroes*. You do see a young father with his son, and the layers of the characters beyond the stern businessman."

Those extra layers were expanded in *Cautionary Tales* when Hiro visited his father in the minutes before his death. "You see that he

"Kaito was very concerned about this weirdo son that he has. In the good Japanese tradition, he wanted Hiro to follow in his footsteps."

loved his wife deeply, and the loss was wrenching to him. You saw that stern facade crumble just a bit," Takei says.

He admits that he didn't really expect to be getting that script, although the show's creator and executive producer had dropped a hint that everything might not be quite as it appeared. "Tim Kring phoned me about a month before the filming on the second season was to begin. He said, 'You may take this to be a Grim Reaper call.' I thought, 'Oh my!' He said there needed to be certainty about certain things, and people needed to be dying off when you have a cast that large. I thought that was it. Then he did indicate that the script I would be getting would get me very deeply concerned… but then said, 'Nothing in *Heroes* is as it seems on the surface.'"

When Takei received the script for *Four Months Later,* he read the scene in which a hooded figure runs at Kaito and they fall off the edge of the Deveaux building. "There is that figure down there and he's wearing the same overcoat that I am," he remembers reading. "An actor always clings to every shred of hope – maybe somehow my overcoat got transferred in the struggle falling down, my power is revealed and I walk away… But that was not to be. That body was me. I realized that as Malcolm McDowell did, and others have done, I would be looking back fondly on the character of Kaito Nakamura."

Resigned to returning to being a viewer of – rather than contributor to – the show, Takei was pleasantly surprised when he received the script for *Cautionary Tales*. "That was a wonderful, delicious script. As an actor, those are the opportunities and the dimensioning that you love, and you so rarely get in series television. It was a surprise: you get into some core human emotions there. It was a challenge, and I love challenges. To get that kind of challenge with a character in series television was an extraordinary blessing."

Of course there are plenty of opportunities for further flashbacks, given how key Kaito Nakamura has been to events in the *Heroes* universe. "When I'm a vigorous young man, Kaito is not being played by me," Takei points out. "Eijiro Ozaki is a very good-looking young actor. He wanted to meet with me. He felt that part of the preparation of getting to know the character was getting to know me. I assured him that he had to have confidence in his own talent. I trusted that he had seen other episodes with Kaito Nakamura in, and he would take from that what he would as an artist, but he had to use his own tools to portray Kaito as a young businessman starting up, and part of The Company in the *Heroes* universe."

But Takei doesn't rule out a reappearance himself. "That's the tantalizing part of *Heroes*!"

Photo: Quang Le

PARTNER IN TIME

NOT ALL THE HEROES IN *HEROES* HAVE GOT POWERS – BUT THAT DOESN'T MAKE THEM ANY LESS INTERESTING. ANDO, HIRO'S TRUSTED COMPANION, HAS HAD MANY ESCAPADES ON THE SHOW, AND LOOKS SET TO HAVE MANY MORE...
ACTOR JAMES KYSON LEE TALKS ALL ABOUT MR. MASAHASHI...

James Kyson Lee has become known to audiences the world over as Ando Masahashi, a Tokyo office worker swept into unexpected adventures by his best friend, Hiro. Lee was born in Seoul, South Korea, and raised in New York City, where his parents moved when he was six. Although he's just put in a 15-hour night working on an episode for season three of *Heroes* – he explains, "We were just shooting one episode, but we were trying to shoot four scenes, and it was these big set-ups, and there was a lot going on" – he is still up for a talk about all things Ando...

Did you always want to be an actor?

JAMES KYSON LEE: When I was a kid, when I was asked what I wanted to do as an adult, I would say, 'President or movie star.' And it's funny I said that, because I was born in Korea and I didn't know any actors. It's not something that you talk about or aspire to. Even when I was growing up in New York City, we didn't know anyone who was a performer. So I don't think it became even a possibility until I moved out to L.A. seven years ago. I didn't know a single thing about acting or Hollywood. I didn't even know what a résumé was, I'd never taken an acting class, and I didn't know anyone here [in Los Angeles], so it was really a crazy world for me (*laughs*). It was a little daunting. But it worked out.

How did you get your first acting job?

My first two years in L.A. were all about learning. I was taking musical theatre and jazz-singing and dance and acting classes for the first time. I felt like I was rediscovering myself, I felt like a kid all over again. I was working as a performer in educational theatre; I did shows for students in the L.A. public schools. It was great. My first [TV] gig was *JAG*, which was on CBS. It was actually my first TV audition. It was for a guest-starring role. And

Photo: Quang Le

Photo: Quang Le

LEE'S LIFE

A look at James Kyson Lee's life and TV/film career

James Kyson Lee was born on December 13 in Seoul, South Korea. His family moved to New York when he was 10. Lee headed to L.A. in 2001, where he began training in jazz-singing, musicals, improv, comedy, and acting.

Lee's first TV break was on the CBS drama *JAG*, and he's been working non-stop ever since. He has appeared in such shows as *The West Wing*, *Las Vegas*, and *Threat Matrix*, while he has taken on movie roles in films like *Big Dreams Little Tokyo*, *Asian Stories (Book 3)*, *Shutter*, *Necrosis*, *Termination Shock*, and *Destiny*.

[my agent] had to tell them, 'This is James' first thing, so he's not even in the Union yet.' So CBS actually paid a fee to "Taft-Hartley" me, which is where you bring a person in [to join the Screen Actors Guild].

What were you told about the character of Ando when you went in to audition for *Heroes*?

They weren't even auditioning anyone for Ando at the time, because they were trying to cast the main nine characters. So I actually auditioned as Hiro, which is really funny, because obviously, me and Masi Oka [who was eventually cast as Hiro] couldn't look more different. I just went with my own interpretation of the character, which was a young man who just wanted to escape the corporate life. I could relate to that experience – I had that [in real life] right after college. I guess they saw something that they liked in me and so the audition process just kept going. I ended up auditioning five times. When it was all over, they said, 'That guy's going to be Hiro and you're going to be Ando.' So they just offered the part to me – they didn't audition a single actor for the part. I guess I was a little disappointed [not to be cast as Hiro], but at the same time, I was intrigued, because there wasn't really anything revealed about Ando yet. All we had was the pilot script, and I knew that he and Hiro were in it together quite a bit. Once the show started, people responded to Ando and Hiro's storyline in such a way that it organically just started to grow.

The photography on the first two spreads and on the bottom right of the next spread is by photographer Quang Le. Quang took the *Heroes* theme and used it to show a comical side of the 'everyday hero'. To see more of Quang's photography, check out www.photosalaquang.com

"PEOPLE ARE ALWAYS ASKING: 'IS ANDO GETTING A POWER?' 'WHEN IS HE GETTING A POWER?' 'I THINK HE'S GETTING A POWER!'"

Photo: Quang Le

FREEZING ANDO

It's not easy playing the best friend of someone who can stop time...

"I'm in a lot [of shots where time freezes]," James Kyson Lee laughs. "I've had shots where I've literally had to look frozen for about 10 seconds or more. It doesn't sound that hard, but it actually is! On camera, every little twitch will come out. You literally have to feel the camera coming your way and then take that final breath. I had some takes, I think it was in season two, where tears started coming out of my eyes during the take – it was just a biological reaction to what was going on, so it was funny."

Lee says as far as he knows, he's never flubbed a take where Ando has to be frozen in time. "If I have [breathed during the shot], it was when the camera was not on me. They actually say I'm one of the best ones on the show at freezing! I don't think that's true, but I have had to do quite a bit of it..."

> "MASI OKA AND I HAVE COMPLETELY DIFFERENT PERSONALITIES. BUT WHEN WE ARE ON THE SCREEN TOGETHER, THERE'S SOMETHING THAT KIND OF DRAWS YOU IN."

I think when we started filming the show, they hinted that I was going to be in at least the first five episodes. I think it was in episode three where I go to New York, [which was] a bit of a foreshadowing that we were embarking on some kind of adventure. I didn't know how long it was going to last, and I tried not to assume anything. Ando has some close calls in season one and there were some times, like in the bus station, when Hiro says, "It's getting too dangerous and you should go back to Japan." I wasn't sure if that was it for the character. But then they brought Ando right back in the next episode, saving the day and coming in as a security guard (*laughs*).

Were you worried Ando was going to die when he went after Sylar with the sword?
It was cool [to have the sword], but yeah, I did think, "So what does this mean?" I remember as I was reading the script, I was really curious to find out how this was going to all end. But it all worked out. Even though I'm a regular cast-member, I never try to assume how long this journey's going to be. I try to just go with what's happening now and just enjoy the moment.

Did you and Masi Oka sense how much your characters were clicking, or was the audience reaction to Ando and Hiro a surprise to you?

I don't know if it was a surprise. We seem to have something going on on-screen. I still don't know how to quite explain it, because in real life, Masi and I have completely different personalities. But when we are on the screen together, there's something – I don't know what it is, but it kind of draws you in. Maybe it's all about the right timing of things. He and I come from different places. Whatever it is, I think we balance each other out and they've been able to play with our storyline a lot, using different types of humor and different elements, whether it's physical comedy or drama and the idea of friendship. [We've been] compared to some fun duos in the past –

Abbott and Costello and Martin and Lewis – and I feel like we're carving out our own identities in the process.

We never discuss [scenes beforehand]. Usually, when we show up to work, we're dressed and ready to go. There's no time for table-reads [actors going over dialogue together before filming]. We rehearse while they're preparing the cameras. So things move very fast and I think that's what keeps it fresh. That's what really fascinates me about the whole chemistry and the comedic timing, because everything that you've seen on-screen pretty much happened spontaneously right there. Maybe it's good that it's not [very] rehearsed, because a lot of comedy comes from truth and being organic and there's a sense of freshness and awe and childlike wonder with our characters, and I think part of that comes from just going with whatever's happening at the moment.

How do you think Ando has changed during his time on *Heroes*?
Ando started with a purpose of

complementing and balancing out Hiro's storyline, and somewhere down the line, he started forming his own identity. I think you'll probably see more of that in season three, where he carves out his own way. It's sort of like this Luke Skywalker/Han Solo relationship. With these guys, I think they go on these adventures together, but their lives are starting to form their own layers and I think that's what makes it interesting.

In the second season, they tried [separating Ando and Hiro for part of the season]. When Hiro went back to the past in Japan, I think a lot of people just felt that when they're not together, something's lacking. When they brought us back together, it really started working again, and I think that's going to carry on through the third season.

Was it difficult to learn Japanese?
I took Japanese in college, but obviously, for the show, I had to study at a whole different level, so once the show started, I had a coach and we were studying the language 50 hours per

Photo: Eric Blackmon – www.ericblackmon.com

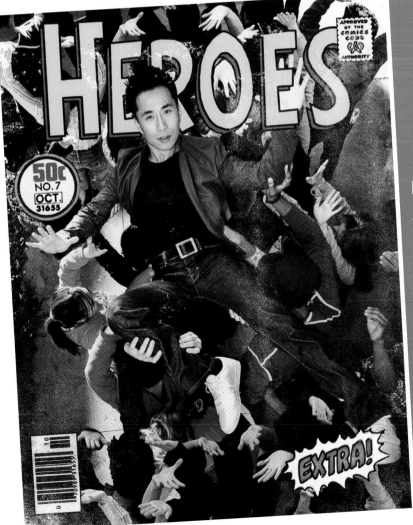

"I ACTUALLY AUDITIONED AS HIRO, WHICH IS REALLY FUNNY, BECAUSE OBVIOUSLY, ME AND MASI OKA COULDN'T LOOK MORE DIFFERENT."

MORE *HEROES*

James Kyson Lee likes the fact that the *Heroes* experience extends far beyond the TV screen...
"It's one of those shows where you can really connect with the fans through different mediums. People want to talk about it the day after, and there's a whole interactive element on the web, and there are graphic novels and now there are trading cards and action figures and video-games. So it's become sort of this whole world and I think when people are able to look back at this show in the future, it will make a mark in pop culture in some way. I would love to [be involved with the video-game version of Ando]. It's my character, so I would like to voice it myself. I think seeing yourself in a video-game has got to be a high point, especially for a guy. I haven't read all of the graphic novels, but Ando was the subject of two of them, where he had a little adventure with Hiro's sister. I read that, and those were really funny."

Photo: Quang Le

EXTRA-CURRICULAR ANDO

James Kyson Lee is pretty busy when he's not playing Ando...

Projects Lee has filmed during *Heroes'* hiatuses include the lead as a "space bandit" in *Termination Shock* for SciFi Channel, the horror film *Necrosis* (pictured right) and a Rastafarian[!] in *Heartbreakers*. "I really enjoy little getaways like that, very different from Ando and just a different environment. As much as I love my job, it's nice to have those opportunities where you go and play and do something completely different."

What Lee sounds happiest about, though, is meeting basketball star Michael Jordan. "When I was growing up, because I love and play a lot of sports, Michael Jordan was the guy I watched constantly. And I got invited to his charity golf tournament, in the Bahamas, of all places. That's like a boy's dream come true. You're going to the Bahamas and meeting Michael Jordan and playing golf. You're pinching yourself at that point."

Is Jordan a *Heroes* fan? "Yeah, he likes the show," Lee laughs. "That's why I was invited."

Necrosis photos: Erié Blackmon

"I THINK IN SOME SENSE ANDO REPRESENTS THE AUDIENCE MEMBER. HE'S THE MORTAL ON THIS SHOW."

(*Laughs*) I've had that happen a lot. Actually, when I was in Japan last year for a movie called *Shutter*, the director was speaking in Japanese. I said, "Hey, you've got to slow down – it's not my native language." Everyone there thought I was [Japanese] because of the show. And I'm not close to [being able to speak quickly in conversational Japanese], because being in a foreign conversation is completely different from studying for a character. But I'm improving on that a lot over the past three years, thanks to the show. It's hard work, but this is the stuff that I really enjoy as an actor, when you're able to work hard on a part using new skills and put on new clothes, if you will, as the character.

How has the fan response been for you and Ando?

episode. When you're speaking that much dialogue, memorizing [phonetic lines] just doesn't work. When you have a line here or there, that's one thing, but it's different when you're playing a character from Japan, who's immersed in this language, right from the beginning. So when we get the script, we get it in English. Me and my coach start with a rough translation. And then I have to read the entire episode straight through to figure out what's going on with the storyline and the arc. Then we break it scene by scene, and then every scene, we break it word by word. That's because there are so many idioms and phrases and sayings in [English], and in

Japanese, it's the same. You can't translate things literally most of the time; you have to understand the context of what's being said and then think about what's being said in today's world. Also, these characters are from Tokyo, and then Ando speaks a very different way than Hiro does. Like in English, we have [phrases] like, 'Hey, what's going on?' 'Oh, boy, crazy day.' Japanese has a whole different cultural aspect that's different from English, and how I speak to Hiro is different from how I address his father, or even his sister. So we discuss every single word and then we talk about how things should be said and why. And then after that, we put everything together, and I work on the intonations and the accent, because Japanese has its own cadence and rhythm that's very different from English and any of the other Asian languages as well. So you can imagine what I'm doing when I'm not filming. This is the hardest I've ever had to work.

Do you have native Japanese speakers coming up to you and start talking in Japanese?

Really good. It seems like a lot of people like the character. I think in some sense he represents the audience member. He's used a lot to bring the audience on the journey – he's like the mortal on this show, and I think that people [like] that there are a lot of elements of loyalty and friendship. They're always asking, though: "Is he getting a power?" "When is he getting a power?" "I think he's getting a power." (*Laughs*) So everybody's got their own theories.

Before we go, is there anything else you'd like to add?

I just want to say thanks to the fans – [their support] really means a lot to me and all of us. This show, probably more than so many other shows, is really fan-driven. I think that's why we feel so connected to how people respond. I think this season is going to be something a lot of people can look forward to and I'm very excited, because we're just getting started. ☽

POWERS TO THE PEOPLE

A LOOK AT THE SPECIAL ABILITIES IN *HEROES*

Ever since Dr. Chandra Suresh published his controversial bestseller, *Activating Evolution*, scientists within the *Heroes'* universe have been puzzling over the Hero gene. Why do some powers manifest themselves so catastrophically, while others need a helping hand? Are powers hereditary? How long has the Hero gene been around?

Here is what has been revealed in the show's first two seasons...

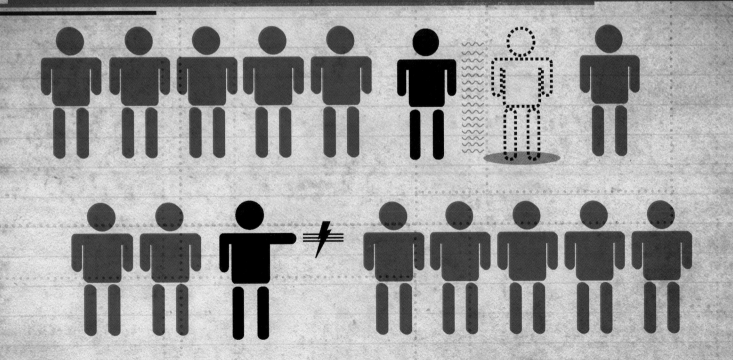

PART ONE – THE HERO GENE

"They say that man uses only a tenth of his brain power. Another percent, and we might actually be worthy of God's image. Unless, of course, that day has already arrived. Teleportation, levitation, tissue regeneration. Is this outside the realm of possibility? Or is man entering a new gateway to evolution? Is he finally standing at the threshold to true human potential?"

In his bestselling book, *Activating Evolution,* scientist Dr. Chandra Suresh poses the question, "What else could the human brain achieve with the subtlest changes in biochemistry?" before going on to describe a genetic marker, known as the Hero gene, which he believes gives ordinary people extraordinary powers. In the same work, Suresh identifies the DNA markers that indicate Hero ability, and even goes as far as developing a mathematical formula to track the marker and locate every single Hero on the planet. His findings are so controversial that he is quickly silenced, leaving his son Professor Mohinder Suresh to take over his research. In a lecture a year after his father's murder, Mohinder describes those that have these abilities as "humanity's evolutionary advancement". He believes that without them and their evolving abilities, the human race has little hope of saving itself.

PART TWO – NATURAL SELECTION

"When evolution selects its agents, it does so at a cost. It makes demands in exchange for singularity. And you may be asked to do something against your very nature. Suddenly, the change in your life that should have been wonderful comes as a betrayal. It may seem cruel, but the goal is nothing short of self-preservation. Survival."

Fig1. Freezing   Fig2. Phasing though Solids
Fig3. Healing Touch   Fig4. Invisibility

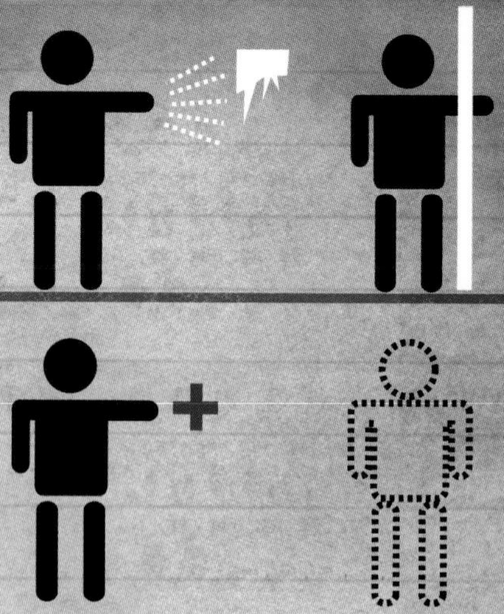

One of the biggest questions surrounding the Hero gene is how long it's been around. Chandra considered himself an atheist, and Mohinder is something of an agnostic, but both sometimes speak as if they believe in a hidden purpose that has made the Heroes' powers start emerging now, just when the world is in dire straits. This belief is far more like some theory of "intelligent design" than science, especially the advanced scientific understanding of DNA and natural selection the two geneticists would have. But in fact, both father and son could be wrong in their belief that these powers are new in evolutionary terms. They are not even the first to study the Heroes, as Mohinder, at least, has already discovered. The Company has been studying the powers, and the Heroes themselves, for at least a generation before Chandra isolated their DNA.

But what if the Hero gene is far, far older than either the geneticists or The Company

scientists believe? Unless Takezo Kensei is a time traveler too, Hiro's discovery that his idol can regenerate proves the Hero DNA has existed in human beings for centuries. More likely, this gene has been handed down in human DNA for thousands of years, or even perhaps has always been there. If people in earlier epochs had Hero powers, most would probably have hidden them, as today's Heroes do. Those Heroes of ancient history who revealed their powers would at best be regarded as gods, and at worst as witches or madmen. Small wonder then that they'd keep them quiet, if the revelation resulted in being burned at the stake. And stories about their powers, like the legends of Takezo Kensei, would be dismissed by the rational and by later generations as myth and folktale. It takes the most innovative science of the 21st Century to bridge the gulf between science and myth.

WHO'S GOT THE POWER?

A handy chart of all the known Hero powers in the series

Volume One Powers	Original Hero	Sylar	Peter
			Who Has It Now?
Flight	Nathan Petrelli		Peter
Empathy	Peter Petrelli		Peter
Regeneration	Claire Bennet		Peter
Teleportation/time control	Hiro Nakamura		Peter (from Future Hiro)
Telepathy	Matt Parkman		Peter
Precognition	Isaac Mendez	Sylar	Peter (from Isaac)
Telekinesis	Brian Davis	Sylar	Peter (from Sylar)
Nuclear/electromagnetic power	Ted Sprague	Sylar	Peter (from Ted)
Technology interface	Micah Sanders		Peter
Super-strength	Niki/Jessica Sanders		Peter
Phasing through solids	D.L. Hawkins		Peter
Clairvoyance	Molly Walker		Peter
Persuasion	Eden McCain		
Eidetic Memory	Charlie Andrews	Sylar	Peter (from Sylar)
Healing touch	Daniel Linderman		
Superhearing	Dale Smither	Sylar	Peter (from Sylar)
Freezing	Unknown	Sylar	Peter (from Sylar)
Radio/wireless interface	Hana Gitelman		
Dreamwalking	Sanjog Iyer		
Pyrokinesis	Meredith Gordon		
Power suppression/memory alteration	The Haitian		
Liquification/molecular control	Zane Taylor	Sylar	Peter (from Sylar)
Invisibility	Claude		Peter
Mastering complex systems	Gabriel Gray (Sylar)	Sylar	Peter (from Sylar)
Illusion generation	Candice Wilmer	Sylar (not yet manifested)	

Volume Two Powers			
Flight	West		
Copycat (mimic)	Monica Dawson		
Midas touch (metal to gold)	Bob		
Killing/Healing	Maya & Alejandro		
Telepathy (advanced)	Maury Parkman		
Regeneration	Takezo Kensei		
Electricity	Elle		

• Peter acquired many of his powers from Sylar, in *Homecoming*, *Parasite*, and *.07%*. At Kirby Plaza, Peter gained new powers from four Heroes: Niki/Jessica, D.L., Micah, and Molly.

• Molly Walker's father James may have been the source of Sylar's freezing power, since his decapitated corpse was the only one of Sylar's victims to be found frozen.

• Shanti Suresh probably had a latent power, as the virus that killed her only infects those with the Hero gene. Since powers run in families, this suggests that Mohinder also may have some latent power. Perhaps it is connected with his blood's ability to cure the virus.

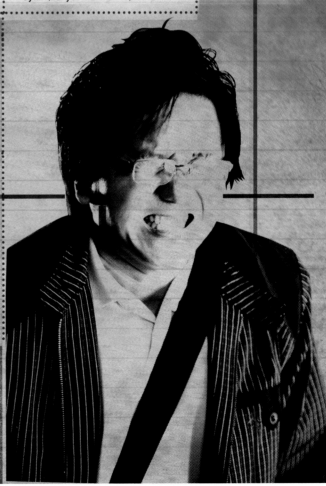

"So much struggle for meaning, for purpose and in the end we find it only in each other. How we share experience of the fantastic and the mundane. The simple human need to find a kindred, to connect and to know in our hearts... that we are not alone."

Seemingly, the powers are hereditary. Or rather, the possibility of having a power is hereditary, since many second-generation Heroes have different powers than those of their parents. Some of today's Heroes seem to be the first in their families to develop powers, while others, like Matt Parkman and the youngest Heroes (Molly, Claire, Micah) are second-generation. Claire may even be third-generation, since her biological grandparents seem to have had powers as well.

Dozens of different powers have already emerged and been identified in the Heroes' universe, and the possibilities seem as infinite as the varieties of human DNA. So far, we have seen two powers duplicated: Claire's regenerative power also appears in Takezo Kensei, while Nathan's power of flight has shown up in the much younger West as well. Do some of these duplicated powers provide an evolutionary advantage that has made them more common? Nathan was skeptical at first that his power of flight had any real use, since he had no other powers to back it up with. There's no denying it has come in useful though, whether it's escaping from Mr. Bennet and The Haitian in his pyjama pants, or flying his exploding kid brother into the stratosphere. West, meanwhile, is unlikely even to ask the question; he knows that being able to fly is just plain cool!

It's easy to see the evolutionary value of Claire's regenerative powers. Just as lizards that can regrow limbs have a biological advantage in survival, the power of complete regeneration virtually guarantees that a human will survive to reproduce the gene that provides this advantage. But here's where natural selection no longer applies, since specific powers, as already noted, are not necessarily passed on to descendants. Claire's father can fly, her mother can start fires, but she can do neither, and neither of them have been seen to regenerate. Micah's father and mother also have totally different powers from his own. So far, Matt Parkman is the only Hero we know who has directly inherited the same power as his parent.

Fig1. Flight Fig2. Empath Fig3. Super-strength Fig4. Nuclear/Electromagnetic Power

HOW TO MAKE MONEY WITH YOUR HERO POWERS

Freezing: Ice cream and frozen foods industries; maintaining ski resorts in the tropics
Teleportation: High speed global courier; travel facilitator to the rich
Melting Metal: Recycling and reclamation; robbing armored cars!
Super-hearing: Intelligence gathering; earthquake prediction
Flying: Bird behavior, migration specialist; meteorology/storm chasing
Precognition: Public safety, emergency preparedness department; futures investments; lottery prediction
Eidetic memory: Research facilitator; gambler
Clairvoyance: Missing persons; law enforcement; fugitive locating
Persuasion: Politician
Midas touch: No job needed!

PART FOUR – MIND OVER MATTER

"In the beginning, there was discovery. A confusion of elements, the first snowfall of impossible change. Old lives undone, left behind. Strange faces made familiar, new nightmares to challenge sleep, new friends to feel safe with. Only then comes control. The need to impose order onto chaos, through determination, through study, through struggle – all in defiance of a thundering truth. They're here. And the earth shudders underfoot."

Is it possible that the individual brain has something to do with how powers manifest? If DNA were all that mattered, Sylar could probably just take any bit of his target's tissue to acquire his powers. His interest in their brains however suggests that there might be some special process in the brain that affects how powers mature, and turns a latent power into an active one.

Peter's evolution gives a hint of how this might work. Mohinder says Peter's DNA mutates to mimic the powers of any Hero he meets. And Peter finds at first that he can only use another's power while he is with that person, in other words, while the new genetic sequence is at its strongest. It's only when Claude throws Peter off a roof – as part of his highly individual form of training! – that Peter discovers how to maintain his powers. He has only seconds to heal himself, or to

die from the fall, so he thinks about Claire – and regenerates. There's a connection between conscious thought and control or manifestation of the powers.

However, the mind/ability connection goes deeper than the conscious mind. Peter hasn't yet used many of his powers, most likely because he is not yet aware that he has them. But his subconscious mind is already learning to draw on any power that he has. When he wakes up in Ireland, he has no memory of his powers or the people he absorbed them from. Yet he phases his wrists through his bonds à la D.L., heals himself like Claire, throws Ted's radioactive whammy, and wields Isaac's paintbrush and Sylar's stolen telekinesis. His amnesia has knocked down the barrier of conscious awareness, and allowed his subconscious to draw on whatever ability he needs.

"When we embrace what lies within, our potential has no limit. The future is filled with promise, the present, rife with expectation. But when we deny our instinct, and struggle against our deepest urges, uncertainty begins. Where does this path lead? When will the changes end? Is this transformation a gift? Or a curse? And for those who fear what lies ahead, the most important question of all: can we ever really change what we are?"

The most interesting aspect of the powers is that each one seems to have almost infinite capacity. When we first see a power manifesting in an emerging hero, what appears seems to be the most undeveloped version of it. Throughout Volume One, Matt Parkman's telepathy seems to be no more than the power to hear the thoughts of others nearby. Then Matt meets his father, Maury, whose first reaction to the news of Matt's power is a non-plussed, "What did you say?" Clearly, Maury's power began in the same simple way. But Maury soon reveals how much more he has learned to do with his gift. He traps Matt and Nathan in their own personal nightmares, so cleverly that they are soon trying to kill each other.

And that's just the beginning. Molly has said all along that "the Nightmare Man" can see her if she looks for him. Maury can also sense the touch of another person's mind from hundreds of miles away, and reach out to attack that person's mind, as he attacked Matt and Nathan. In light of this power, and his apparent intention to attack Bob next, it even seems possible that Maury was also Angela Petrelli's invisible attacker in the police station, making her think something or someone was attacking her, and only battering herself as she tried to fight him off.

Other powers have been seen to expand this way, as the Heroes grow accustomed to them. Claire must have started testing her healing powers with small injuries before she tried jumping off a tower, or at least we'd hope so. Soon she successfully regenerates from fatal head trauma, impalement on a branch and the resulting autopsy, and even near incineration. Then she takes it yet another step. When her biology professor shows a video of a lizard re-growing a limb, Claire tries a gruesome experiment (being now completely accustomed to the sight of her own blood and worse) and finds that she has the lizard's talent: the toe she severs grows back in seconds. If she can re-grow a limb, and if Peter, with the same power, can survive his own thermonuclear detonation, we might well ask if even a deadly disease would faze these two, or if their cells can regenerate faster than

any pathogen can destroy them.

Not all powers start small. When some powers first manifest, they are already too big, too dangerous, and too uncontrolled. Maya kills everyone near her every time she gets frightened, while Ted's nuclear ability is so vast and deadly that it can irradiate whatever he approaches (just ask his late wife…), or even level a city. Yet even Ted's power doesn't have to be cataclysmic. It too can be focused. With practice and guidance, Ted learns how to control his power precisely enough to send a targeted EMP through a building's electrical systems, or heat up a frozen car engine just enough to jump-start it. From Ted, we can extrapolate that Maya and Alejandro could also learn to control their powers and use them not only more constructively, but also with precision, in ways we can't yet begin to guess, because we don't yet understand the nature of their abilities.

Why do some powers start small, while others start large? Hiro starts by making a subway train 14 seconds late, and teleporting into a ladies' restroom. His power could have just as easily begun at the opposite, cosmic extreme, teleporting him to the ends of the universe and time, or stopping the entire solar system in its orbit. Luckily for him, and the universe, that didn't happen. If Micah's power had started big too, he might have crashed the entire national banking system when he hacked one ATM. Whether a power first manifests in a small or big way seems to be fairly random. Starting small is probably an evolutionary advantage (overwhelming power might kill a Hero before he learned to use it); but if the Hero gene has only just begun to appear ("just" being a relative term in human evolution), then natural selection probably hasn't had nearly enough generations to weed out the genes of Heroes whose powers start big.

THE HERO PLAGUE

Who discovered it? Chandra Suresh first identified the virus, when his young daughter Shanti contracted it.
Who can catch it? The virus only attacks those with the hero DNA. After Shanti, only two other individuals have caught it: Molly Walker, and The Haitian.
What are the symptoms? Weakness, tremors, loss of abilities, death.
How can it be treated? Antibodies processed from Mohinder's blood are the only known cure.
How contagious is it? Not very – at least, not yet. However, it is so virulent that Bob is afraid it may mutate and cross over into the general population. Mohinder is more afraid that the virus will render the Heroes extinct before they can save the world.

PART SIX – THE HERO EMERGES

"What happens when the familiar becomes unsafe? When the fear that we have been desperately trying to avoid finds us where we live? We are all, at our cores, the sum of our fears. To embrace destiny, we must, inevitably, face those fears and conquer them, whether they come from the familiar or the unknown."

Another question that has not yet been addressed is why some Heroes discover their powers as children, while the powers of others may not emerge until well into adulthood. Perhaps, in children and adults, the power is always there, latent, waiting for the mind to mature enough to control it, and waiting for the need to bring it out. Peter's power begins with dreaming that he can fly. Because he has been spending time with his flying brother, this might be his subconscious mind telling him what he can now do. The powers of some other Heroes emerge when they need them most, like when Nathan flies away from a car accident. For some, the need is more mundane: Hiro's desire to be special; Matt's frustration with his dead-end life, failing his detective exams, and drifting away from his wife. For others, like Ted and Maya, it may never be clear why their powers emerged so catastrophically.

Most Heroes have to practice to develop their powers. The exception is Sylar, who shows a quick and deadly aptitude with his stolen powers. His original power, of understanding and controlling complex systems, is probably the key to this. He had only to look into his first victim's brain to understand how to take his telekinetic power; and by the next day was well on his way toward mastering it, though his victim, Brian, had barely been able to use it.

Because of his gift for understanding, Sylar may understand better than any other Hero, and better than anyone studying the powers, just how the powers work. This is bad news for anyone fighting him. However, Peter now also has Sylar's power of understanding how things work. Added to his experience in using many different powers and his nurturing, empathetic temperament, the combination could someday make Peter the mentor of a whole new generation of Heroes. And that could be very good news for the world.

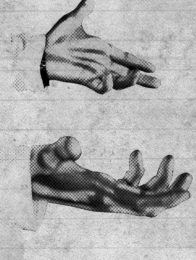

STAR

With his insatiable appetite for power and his terrifying penchant for murder,
Heroes' Sylar is one villain you definitely would not want to meet down a dark
alley. Or by the High School lockers. Or in a café's kitchen. Or anywhere else,
for that matter.
Actor Zachary Quinto talks about being bad…

SYLAR PROFILE

Gabriel Gray followed in his father's footsteps and became a watchmaker in Queens in the family business — but he longed to be special. Thanks to Gray's incredible skills at watch repair, Chandra Suresh, a geneticist researching "special people", thinks he has found someone with an extraordinary talent. Later, when Chandra discovers the talents Gabriel has are learnt and not natural, Gabriel becomes angry because he is not "special" and kills Chandra.

Gabriel starts to call himself Sylar (after a watch manufacturer), and a villain is born. He hunts down people with extraordinary talents (including our Heroes) in order to slice their heads open and steal their brains and powers.

After a lengthy killing spree, Sylar goes head-to-head with the Heroes. During all the commotion of the Petrelli brothers' heroics, Sylar escapes. He wakes up powerless and under guard by Candice, but soon escapes...

I n a world where cheerleaders can heal themselves, nurses can mimic other people's abilities, and Japanese office workers can manipulate the space/time continuum, there isn't much that can harm or even threaten them. Nonetheless, over the course of a season, one word, one man, sent plenty of these characters cowering in terror and running scared. Sylar.

A normal but meek second generation watchmaker from Queens, New York, Gabriel Gray once dreamed of being a bright light in the sky until emerging as *Heroes'* resident boogeyman. Yet despite targeting evolved humans and removing their brains to absorb their powers, this "Patient Zero" proved to be more than just some maniacal serial killer with an unquenchable hunger. Complex, and with his own personal scars, Sylar is the villain viewers can almost sympathize with. Almost. Now the actor behind the menacing stare, Zachary Quinto, discusses Sylar's cruel intentions, killing off his fellow cast-mates, and beaming up onto the latest *Star Trek* movie...

How did you come on board *Heroes*? Was it a difficult audition?
ZACHARY QUINTO: It was a pretty traditional audition process in terms of the experiences I've previously had. It was for an audition I had got from my agents one day. I had been aware of the show because I had read the Pilot and heard it had gotten picked up. At the time, I wasn't available because I was working on another series, but I was really drawn to *Heroes*.

Initially, what kind of discussions did you have with the producers regarding Sylar?
It was, "Where is this guy coming from? How is he going to fit into the world? What are the things that are important for me to keep in mind?" I didn't really need to have too many conversations, because there was so much that was offered to me in terms of the text and what I was given to play with at the very beginning. It was so rich, so I filled in the blanks with the producers – but there weren't that many blanks. The writers have done an amazing job of creating this character and creating him in a way that he had so much history built in the first time that you met him. That helped me out.

That is interesting – a lot of serialized shows don't seem to have all those details mapped out right away.
That's because the first time you meet Sylar is six months in the past, so they had to answer some of those questions – but not all of them. I've certainly answered a number of them for myself. It was a great place to start because the audience had an expectation of what this character should be, or would be, and then in that episode, they totally turned that expectation on its head.

Many of the *Heroes* characters evolved from what was originally outlined on the page. Was that the case with Sylar, too?

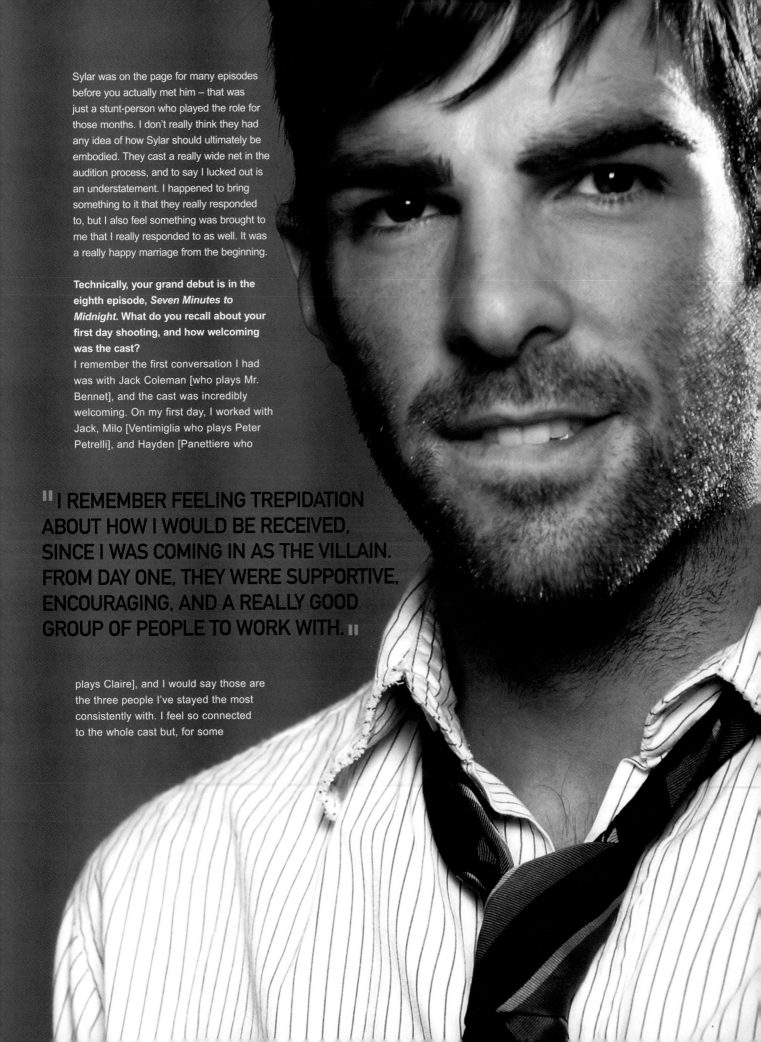

Sylar was on the page for many episodes before you actually met him – that was just a stunt-person who played the role for those months. I don't really think they had any idea of how Sylar should ultimately be embodied. They cast a really wide net in the audition process, and to say I lucked out is an understatement. I happened to bring something to it that they really responded to, but I also feel something was brought to me that I really responded to as well. It was a really happy marriage from the beginning.

Technically, your grand debut is in the eighth episode, *Seven Minutes to Midnight*. What do you recall about your first day shooting, and how welcoming was the cast?
I remember the first conversation I had was with Jack Coleman [who plays Mr. Bennet], and the cast was incredibly welcoming. On my first day, I worked with Jack, Milo [Ventimiglia who plays Peter Petrelli], and Hayden [Panettiere who

❚❚ I REMEMBER FEELING TREPIDATION ABOUT HOW I WOULD BE RECEIVED, SINCE I WAS COMING IN AS THE VILLAIN. FROM DAY ONE, THEY WERE SUPPORTIVE, ENCOURAGING, AND A REALLY GOOD GROUP OF PEOPLE TO WORK WITH. ❚❚

plays Claire], and I would say those are the three people I've stayed the most consistently with. I feel so connected to the whole cast but, for some

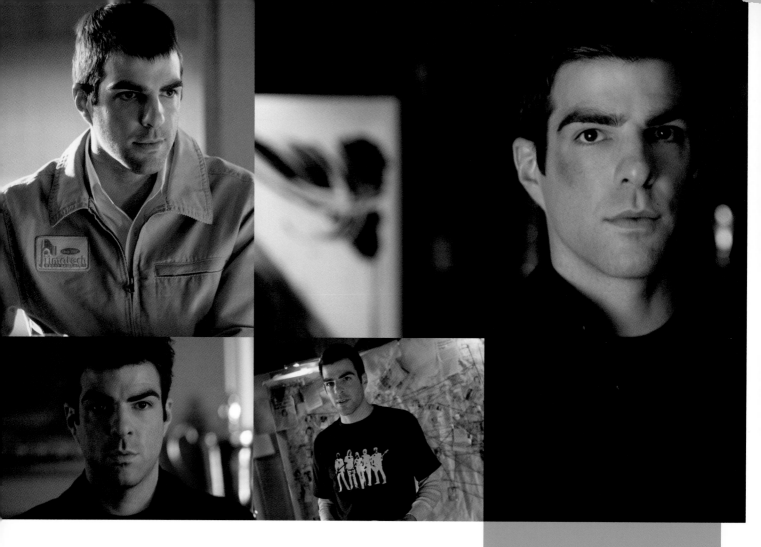

reason, I feel a great connection to those three. I also certainly worked with Milo and Jack quite a bit in the first season. But I remember feeling trepidation about how I would be received, since I was coming in as the villain. From day one, they were supportive, encouraging, and a really good group of people to work with. They've become an extension of my professional family.

What was the key in finding the dark side of Sylar and keeping up the intensity for him?

I certainly have my own doors into that kind of darkness. I don't think we need to look very far in the world we live in to see examples all around us. That is an unfortunate state of affairs, but one I've often been able to draw upon as an actor to enhance the depths of this character. Certainly, many personal perspectives and experiences are drawn upon to understand the motivation of this character because, ultimately, that is all I need to do as an actor. I don't look at it like, "Oh, I must find the darkness within me." I have to find the way in

which someone can be driven to go as far as this character goes, someone who can be hungry enough to make the kind of decisions this character makes along the way.

From week to week, do you feel Sylar had some masterplan, or was he simply insane and power hungry?

I think hunger is the primary underlying motivation for Sylar. Hunger for power, hunger for validation, for approval, for meaning, and for purpose. Those are all the things that drive him. Ultimately, a plan took shape as the season progressed, but I think the masterplan was to acquire as much power as possible. What to do with it then becomes a separate issue.

Did your role as a warlock on *Charmed* prepare you with the hand gestures to bring Sylar's powers to life?

I come from a background in theatre, so I draw on that more than anything else. I've had a good sense of imagination since I was a kid, so when you are in a situation where you have to act to things that aren't even there, which you often are on *Heroes*,

SYLAR TREK

> **"SYLAR IS A LOST SOUL, A SAD, WOUNDED LITTLE GUY. I THINK THERE ARE REDEEMING QUALITIES TO EVERY CHARACTER."**

SELECTED TV CREDITS – ZACHARY QUINTO

So noTORIous – Sasan (2006)
Blind Justice – Scott Collins (2005)
24 – Adam Kaufman (2003–2004)
Dragnet – Howard Simms (2004)
Charmed – Warlock (2003)
Six Feet Under – Art Student (2003)
CSI: Crime Scene Investigation – Mitchell Sullivan (2002)
Touched by an Angel – Mike (2001)
The Others – Tony (2000)

I draw on my theatrical experiences.

Characters such as Niki aren't all hero material. Are there any redeeming qualities to Sylar?
Suuuure… (*laughter*) Yeah, I think there are redeeming qualities to every character. It is part of what I try to stay connected to. He is a lost soul, a sad, wounded little guy. There is redemption in the fact he didn't set out to be as evil as he ultimately became. I don't know. We will see if that gets explored.

How did Sylar's relationship with his mother shape him into the man he is now?

There was big news for Sylar and Zachary Quinto fans recently, as Quinto was cast as Spock for the upcoming *Star Trek* movie. We chatted to the busy actor about how he got the role and his thoughts on the *Star Trek* franchise...

ZACHARY QUINTO: I have known for a while that I had got the Spock role. I knew for six weeks before they made an official announcement. It was a very difficult secret to keep. It was a long, drawn out process of negotiation. Obviously, it is a huge project, to negotiate the terms of that contract, but also to negotiate the schedule, and to get [the *Heroes* people] to let me do it. Tim Kring was behind it from the beginning. He, J.J. Abrams, and Damon Lindelof are basically the three people to whom I ultimately owe gratitude for this. They are totally the ones who made it happen, and Tim and Damon have a long-standing history of working together and they have a long friendship. Tim supported this all the way through and I owe him a lot for that. So it was just a matter of figuring out how to make it work, getting NBC behind it, getting Paramount behind it, and making sure everyone was happy with the availability. The schedule for the movie is going to be pretty demanding, so it's not going to give me time for anything else. I told a few people I was very close to, but I waited until the Tuesday and Wednesday of the week we made the announcement to spread the word to the wider circle of my friends and family so they weren't completely taken by surprise.

Were you a huge Trekkie growing up?
Nope. I was a peripheral fan. I had seen a few episodes and a couple of movies, but I wasn't really into the franchise. I was more drawn to this project because of the characters and the point in their lives that we meet them. I was drawn to the character elements of the story rather than the international success of the franchise.

Have you spoken to the original Spock, Leonard Nimoy, at all?
I've had many cool conversations with that guy. He's endlessly fascinating to me, really intriguing, and a genuine, deep artist. I feel real fortunate to not only have his blessing, but have his involvement in this endeavor. It is going to be enormously helpful and inspiring to work as closely as I already am.

How do you feel about the pointy ears?
I feel good about it. I went and got my head molded last week. They put this plaster all over, smear it all over your head, and you are basically in this helmet where you can only breathe through your nostrils for half an hour. It is kind of freaky. Then they did a silicon cast of my ears to make them. I am really excited to see the technology and how the ears are made and applied. It is going to be a lot of meditating in the chair, since I imagine it is going to be at least an hour and a half between my ears and eyebrows. I'm really looking forward to seeing how the process unfolds. All that stuff is cool; I'm really into that movie magic. It will also really inform the character hugely to actually have the ears and step into the character from a physical perspective and balance out the emotional work I'll be doing leading up to production.

Have you had to practice the Vulcan peace sign?
I am left-handed, so I can only do it on my left, but I do exercises! I rubber-band my ring finger and pinky finger. It is part of my personal training!

He's one of the most chilling villains to hit our TV screens in recent years. Here we look at Sylar's best (or should that be worst?!) episodes…

HOMECOMING (SEASON ONE, CHAPTER 9)
In the climax to the "save the cheerleader" story arc, Sylar is still a mystery in the shadows when he arrives at Claire's high school to steal her powers. Unfortunately for Sylar (but luckily for Claire), he gets the wrong girl and Peter manages to stop him from killing Claire.

FALLOUT (SEASON ONE, CHAPTER 11)
Sylar doesn't take it well when Mr. Bennet captures him and puts him in a cell specially designed to stop him using his powers. Eden tries to use her super-powers of persuasion to get Sylar to commit suicide, but instead ends up paying with her own life.

.07% (SEASON ONE, CHAPTER 19)
Sylar and Peter go head-to-head in this episode; Peter has the ability to take on anyone's power, whilst Sylar can only steal them. This is surely the clash of the Titans, *Heroes*-style! Peter is stabbed with shards of glass after turning invisible – he is wounded, apparently mortally. Just as Sylar's preparing to steal Peter's power, Mohinder crushes him against the wall, knocking him out. When Sylar wakes up, Mohinder has destroyed his list of "special people."

FIVE YEARS GONE (SEASON ONE, CHAPTER 20)
When we go back to the future with Ando and Hiro, we discover that although the President of the United States looks like Nathan Petrelli, something more sinister lurks beneath that wholesome exterior: Sylar! Having attained the power to take on the form of others, Sylar is more powerful than he could have ever dreamed possible back when he was a mere watchmaker.

THE HARD PART (SEASON ONE, CHAPTER 21)
Sylar's back-story in this episode shed a lot of light on what our megalomaniac Sylar's up to and why he's on a mission to steal brains. He was a brilliant watch-mender in New York when Chandra Suresh plucked him from obscurity and told him he was "special". On hearing the news that he's not "special" in Hero terms, Sylar gets mad and goes on a killing spree to gain others' powers.

Well, she's crazy and it rubbed off a little bit. It is interesting. I think his mother really fed his deficit by constantly telling him he was capable of more, that he is more, more, more – which leaves somebody wondering why what they are isn't enough. That is part of what drove him in his pursuit for greater things, and that just turned ugly. When Chandra Suresh walked into the watch store, it opened up a whole new world; it changed the whole picture for him forever.

That scene between Sylar and his mom was so unexpected. Were you happy to be showing that more vulnerable side of him?
I was. That was definitely the most challenging – and more rewarding – episode this season. Working with the incomparable Ellen Greene, the actress who played my mom, was amazing. I was familiar with her before I got to work with her, so that was really exciting for me. Then the themes that

were explored from my character's perspective in that episode were really important. That was a good one for me.

Heroes established these wonderful, conflicted characters throughout the season, so was it difficult when you discovered Isaac would be Sylar's next victim?
That was hard. Santiago [Cabrera] and I had become friends, and I had a lot of respect for him as a person and an actor. It is the unfortunate reality of the show we are on, and an unfortunate role I will probably have to fulfill again at some point down the line. It is a bummer and it is hard because these are your friends and then it becomes about something else. But everybody knows that this is a part of what we are doing, everybody is aware, including myself, that in order to serve the progression of the story and quality of the show, you might have to sacrifice your part in that in order to let it

SYLAR VERSUS PETER

What is your take on the bad blood between Sylar and Peter? Why does Sylar hate him so much?

ZACHARY QUINTO: Peter represents the opposite of Sylar. Peter is complementary in his power. I represent the shadow side and he represents the side of the light, so I'm blinded by him. I love working with Milo [Ventimiglia] and he has fast became one of my favorite people in life and not just on the show.

continue on to a greater life. Nobody handled that greater than Santiago last year, and it was really moving to be in his final scenes as he was leaving the show.

There was a building anticipation for the season one finale. What were your thoughts on that confrontation between Sylar and Peter?

It was a really, really intense thing to shoot. That sequence in Kirby Plaza took a long time to shoot because it involved so many people and was covered from so many

angles. That time was very overwhelming for all of us in terms of the amount of energy we were putting into the show. Everybody was pretty tired by then, because we were right at the end and there were a lot of night shoots. I was really pleased with the season finale and I thought it was emotionally satisfying.

That culminated with this big, epic battle between two forces. Were you concerned this could be the end of Sylar?

Well, no, because by then I was already signed on as a series regular (*laughter*). But every time you open a script, you should be concerned it could be the end of the character. I knew the truth, so we were just misleading the audience.

What has you excited about season two?

Everything. The journey of these characters. I'm excited by the response it is going to generate from people when they see it, because it's so different. The thing our show does best is defy expectations and season two is going to be no exception.

After being wounded and facing these Heroes, how have Sylar's goals changed?

Well, the scope of them has narrowed to really just involve a sense of survival. You'll see what I mean when the season starts.

Were there any Sylar moments that really stood out for you?

The episode with Mohinder called *Run*. It was when we were on our road trip to Virginia and there was the auto-mechanic with the super-hearing. There was something about the shooting of the episode, the work

that I did for the director really resonated with me as one of the more enjoyable episodes of the season. It was really about a connection between these characters and was the most delicious manipulation and deception that Sylar was perpetrating. That was really fun to play.

And *Five Years Gone* gives us a glimpse of what tomorrow could possibly bring.

I was pleasantly surprised that Sylar was President of the United States. If that future comes to pass, I have a lot to look forward to. It was a great episode which my character factored prominently into. But Adrian [Pasdar] got to embody my character for the most part, except for a couple of times when I emerged.

Have you been amazed at what an international hit *Heroes* has become?

Yeah, that is crazy! I went to Paris in April and the show hadn't even aired yet. There is a barrage of people interested in it already.

> "I WAS PLEASANTLY SURPRISED THAT SYLAR WAS PRESIDENT OF THE UNITED STATES. IF THAT FUTURE COMES TO PASS, I HAVE A LOT TO LOOK FORWARD TO."

When people see you in public, what is their general response now? They must know you from *Heroes* and probably that you will be playing Spock in the new *Star Trek* movie.

People are really enthusiastic about the show and the fact I am doing the movie. They've been nothing but supportive and really excited about talking to me. I hope that continues and I am really grateful to meet a lot of interesting, colorful people as a result of my experience. I'm sure that is only going to intensify when I meet the *Star Trek* fans.

Lastly, if Sylar was on the Starship *Enterprise*, who would come out on top – him or Spock?

That is a tough position to put me in, because who would I want to come in first? Good always has to triumph at some point... Or it could be "The Wrath of Sylar"? We'll see... ↻

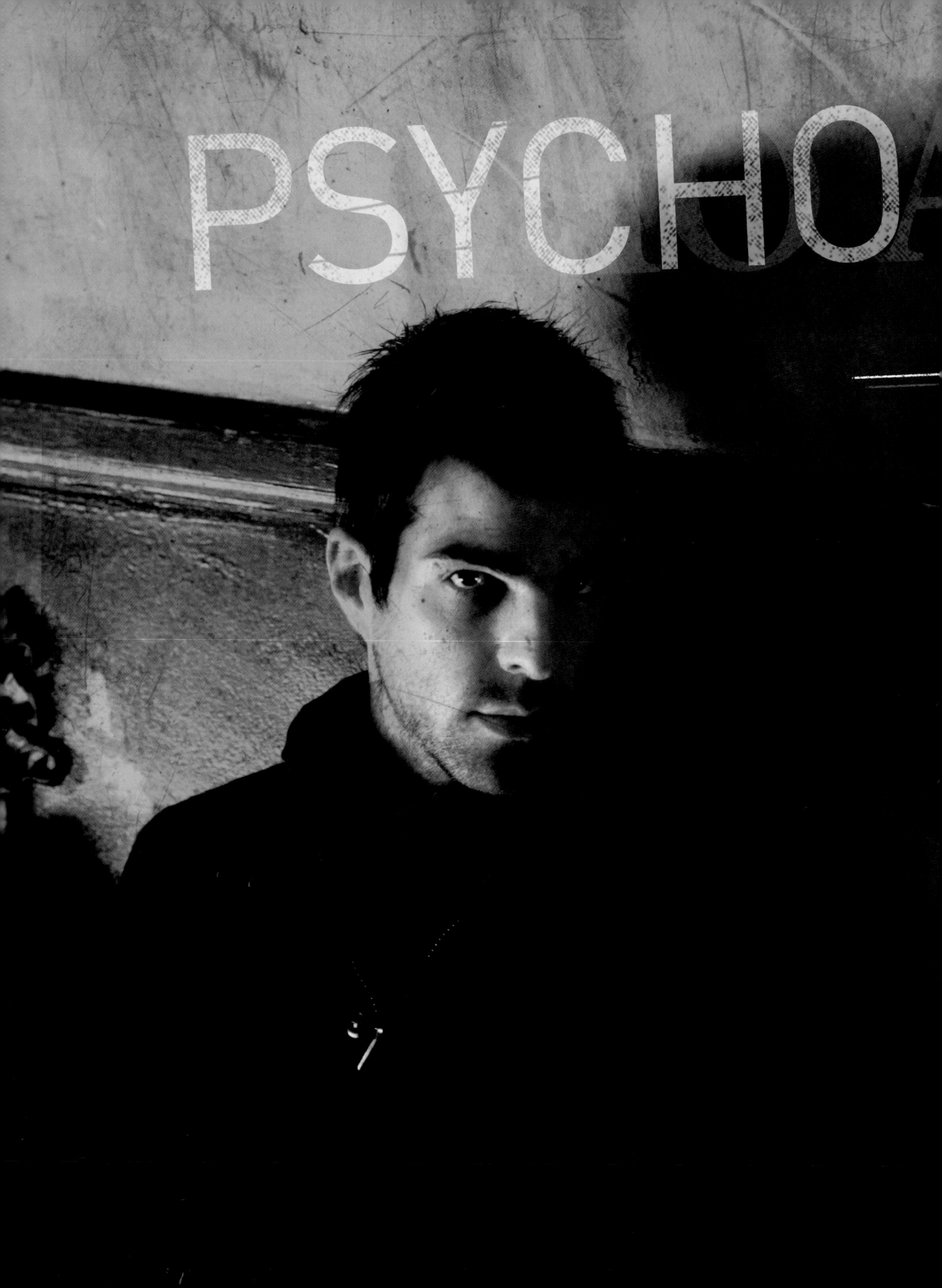
PSYCHO

ANALYSIS

A profile of *Heroes'* Sylar

Chapter 1: Patient Zero

"When I was a kid, I used to wish some stranger would come and tell me my family wasn't really my family. They weren't bad people, they were just... insignificant. And I wanted to be different... special... I wanted to be important."
– Gabriel Gray, *Six Months Ago*

He is a watchmaker, and a son to be proud of. He's orderly, neat, quiet, and loves to read; the walls of his modest apartment are lined with books. He inherited his father's watch repair shop, and has kept it going successfully since his father's death. And ever since he was a child, he has dreamed of being special.

In fact, Gabriel Gray does have a unique talent. He can look at anything complex, from a time-piece to a human brain, and figure out how it works and how to make it work better. At a glance, he diagnoses a problem with Chandra Suresh's watch, and repairs it in less than a minute. He tells Chandra that he has "a talent for the way things work, how the parts should go." But neither Chandra nor Gabriel recognizes this talent as the genesis of a Hero power. And even if they had, perhaps Gabriel wouldn't have been satisfied, after the expectations Chandra has raised. This talent that makes him a good watchmaker is part of his insignificance. And he wants much more. He wants to be extraordinary.

So when Chandra fails to detect anything in his first case-study, Gabriel can't accept the shattering of his great hopes. He goes in search of the powers he craves, tracking down another name on Chandra's list, Brian Davis, who shows him a genuine, extraordinary power: telekinesis. Brian doesn't want this wonderful power, which Gabriel would do anything to have. And that makes it easy for Gabriel. "You're broken," he says, and smashes Brian's head in to take apart his brain and absorb his telekinesis. Sylar is born...

Chapter 2: The Most Special Person There Is

"I'm a natural progression of the species. Evolution is a part of nature, and nature kills. Simple, right?"
– Sylar, *Parasite*

Sylar believes in the evolutionary imperative even more than Gabriel, who says that he became a watchmaker through genetic destiny, not choice – because his father was one. Sylar justifies his first murder – and every murder afterwards – as the birthright of the superior man. Because Brian was afraid of his power, he didn't deserve it. It should go to the man who isn't afraid, who wants the power and knows how to use it.

From Brian, Sylar easily crosses the line to killing anyone with a power, without bothering to find out whether they're using it properly, or whether they "deserve" it more than he does. He rationalizes that he should have all those powers, because he is superior, smarter, more special. And each successful murder reinforces this belief. He deserves the powers more than his victims, partly because he's smart enough, strong enough, and ruthless enough to take them. He's special, so the rules for normal humans don't apply to him.

And sometimes, he doesn't even feel the need for rationalizations. He's having too much fun adding to his growing collection of powers. He calls Maya a "shiny new toy" who is all his, and when he sees Peter turn invisible, he observes, "I can't wait to try that one!" He is, after all, a very intelligent guy, who has a special gift for complex things. It's a pleasure and a thrill for him to discover what each new power can do, to figure out how it works, and to find ways to use it against his victims and his enemies.

SYLAR RATIONALIZES THAT HE SHOULD HAVE EVERYONE'S POWERS BECAUSE HE IS SUPERIOR, SMARTER, MORE SPECIAL. THE RULES FOR NORMAL HUMANS DON'T APPLY TO HIM.

Chapter 3: The Easy Part

"Get away from him. He's a murderer!"
"*I* am a murderer! Gabriel understands exactly what I'm going through – exactly how I feel."
– Alejandro and Maya, *Truth and Consequences*

Though all these stolen powers now make Sylar almost impossible to stop, they are not what makes him a murderer; and he doesn't stop being one when his powers are suppressed by the Shanti virus. He murders his very first victim, Brian Davis, without using any powers, because he hasn't acquired any; and while he's powerless from the virus he commits at least three murders, two of them with his favorite method of bashing the victim's head from behind. Even if he never got his powers back, Sylar could probably go on being a successful murderer for a very long time. He really is superior in many ordinary human abilities: intelligence, cunning, charm, and above all in knowing what makes people tick.

In fact, Sylar has terrific people skills. He's a good listener and a keen observer of human strengths, desires, and weaknesses – especially weaknesses. And he's extremely good at getting people to trust him. His charm is a big part of this ability. Whenever it suits him, he assumes the persona of Gabriel, a nice guy, sincere, humorous, and unusually sympathetic to others. As a watchmaker, he probably *was* a nice guy, and well liked by his customers. As a murderer, his ability to put on a nice persona works so well that he travels for days with Mohinder, and with Maya, Alejandro, and Derek, without raising any suspicion in their minds. The reverse, in fact; the longer he stays with them, the more they like and trust him – particularly Maya.

The seduction of Maya is Sylar's masterpiece. He first wins her friendship by telling her he knows Chandra Suresh, then extends his hold by giving her understanding, support, and reassurance about her terrifying powers. He uses her guilt over the death of her brother's bride to drive a wedge between the siblings. And when Alejandro discovers Sylar is wanted for murdering his mother, Sylar actually uses this revelation to cement the bond between him and Maya, convincing her he has more in common with her than Alejandro does. She trusts him so completely that moments after he murders Alejandro, she literally falls into his arms, never suspecting her brother is dead or that Gabriel would hurt him.

Sylar shows the flip-side of his people skills the minute he has a victim helpless in his power. Then he absolutely delights in gloating over them as he prepares to kill them. Sometimes his gloating is a casual chat with a mild air of interest, as we see when he's preparing to take Peter apart and discover what powers he has. Sometimes it's pure glee, such as when he tells Alejandro exactly what he's planning to do to him and his sister, knowing that Alejandro can't understand a word. He even gloats when he's in someone else's power, as when he brags to Mr. Bennet, from his cell in the Odessa facility, that he's going to kill Claire as soon as he escapes. Whatever he's gloating over, it's all about staying in control, and savoring the feeling of power.

> SYLAR IS A VERY INTELLIGENT GUY, WHO HAS A SPECIAL GIFT FOR COMPLEX THINGS. IT'S A PLEASURE AND A THRILL FOR HIM TO DISCOVER WHAT EACH NEW POWER CAN DO AND TO FIND WAYS TO USE IT AGAINST HIS VICTIMS AND HIS ENEMIES.

Head Count

A list of Sylar's known victims so far...

Killed for their powers:
- Brian Davis, telekinesis. *Six Months Ago*
- Molly Walker's parents, powers unknown, possibly freezing. *Don't Look Back*
- Zane Taylor, liquifaction. *Run*
- Dale Smither, superhearing. *Unexpected*
- Charlie Andrews, perfect memory. *Seven Minutes to Midnight*
- Isaac Mendez, precognition. *.07%*
- Ted Sprague, radioactivity. *Landslide*
- Candice Wilmer, illusion. *Kindred*

Killed because they were in his way:
- Chandra Suresh. *Seven Minutes to Midnight*
- Jackie Wilcox (in mistake for Claire). *Homecoming*
- Hank, Company medical employee. *The Fix*
- Virginia Gray, his mother. *The Hard Part*
- Derek. *The Kindness of Strangers*
- Alejandro Herrera. *Truth and Consequences*

Unknown victims:
A series of killings attributed to him by FBI Agent Audrey Hanson (*Don't Look Back, One Giant Leap*). From some of these victims he must have acquired unidentified powers which allowed him to survive Matt's shooting him in *One Giant Leap*, walk away from his fall in *Homecoming*, and overcome The Company's drugs and Eden's suicide suggestion in *Fallout*.

Chapter 4: The Luxury of Regret

> "Believe me, I understand what you're going through. To be held responsible for things that you didn't mean to do. Being hunted."
> – Sylar to Maya, *The Kindness of Strangers*

Sylar may put on the persona of Gabriel Gray when he needs to, yet somewhere inside him, that nice, sincere, ordinary man survives for months after his first murder. Gabriel's hand decorates the hidden closet Mohinder finds in Sylar's lair: a closet whose walls are covered with the words "FORGIVE ME. I have sinned. Forgive me Father, for I have sinned." He tries to make others complicit in his crimes, to shed some of the guilt and responsibility, leaving messages on Chandra's answering machine, claiming that it's Chandra's fault he's a murderer; and he tells Mr. Bennet that they're alike because "we both collect special people." It's Gabriel who is recognizing guilt, when Sylar tries to share his crimes with others.

Finally, Gabriel emerges again when Sylar foresees that he could be the exploding man who destroys New York. Even the serial killer recoils from the thought of wiping out a whole city. He tells Mohinder that it was "natural selection" for him to kill those who didn't deserve their powers. But this is different. "An apocalypse… Half the city gone in an instant. They mean nothing. They're innocent. There's no gain, so why would I do it? What possible reason could I have for killing so many?"

When Mohinder offers him only the option of turning himself in and repenting, Sylar turns to his mother, hoping that she can give him a way out of the oncoming holocaust, if he can just win her acceptance and understanding. It's a futile hope, as it has been all his life.

This pic: Sylar is captured by The Company in season one; Below left: Sylar confronts his mother – with deadly results…

Chapter 5: The Watchmaker's Son

"You were right, mom. I am meant to be special, just like you wanted. I can be anything. I can even be President."
– Sylar, *The Hard Part*

SYLAR HAS TERRIFIC PEOPLE SKILLS. HE'S A GOOD LISTENER AND A KEEN OBSERVER OF HUMAN STRENGTHS, DESIRES AND WEAKNESSES – ESPECIALLY WEAKNESSES.

Though Virginia Gray only appears for a few minutes, in that time her words and gestures write a whole biography of her relationship with her son. She wants her boy to be "special," by which she means rich and important. It isn't enough for her that he became a watchmaker like his father, and took over the family business. She calls Gabriel's profession – her late husband's profession – a "hobby," and tells her son (probably for about the millionth time) that he should get a lucrative job such as being an investment banker. She apparently didn't value her husband either: when Gabriel notices that his father's antique clock has stopped working, she calls it "junk" and says she wants to throw it out. Clearly, it was Virginia who taught Gabriel to think that his family was insignificant.

Virginia is so caught up in her ideas of who she wants Gabriel to be, that she doesn't listen to what he actually wants or needs. When he tells her that he might have to hurt a lot of people in order to become special, she doesn't even take in his fear or the trouble he's obviously in. He's her son, so he has to be perfect, and she just brushes aside his statement. Finally, Gabriel – Sylar – asks her the most important question of his life: "Maybe I don't have to be special. That's okay – to just be a normal watchmaker. Can't you just tell me that's enough?"

It's the only moment in the whole story when we feel sorry for him, and think of him more as Gabriel than Sylar. And Gabriel's mother refuses to tell him that normal is okay. She needs to believe that her boy can be important, famous, rich. The ways that Gabriel the watchmaker was special – kindness, his ability to listen, his remarkable talent for fixing things – those aren't enough for her. She loves what she wants her son to be, not Gabriel himself. And when he reveals who he has become, the man with remarkable powers that can hurt as well as delight, she denies that he's her son, attacks him, and is killed in the struggle.

Hero/Anti-Hero

Besides Sylar, only Peter Petrelli has absorbed multiple powers.
How do Sylar and his opposite compare?

PETER	SYLAR
• Acquires powers naturally, absorbing them like a sponge, without harming the other Hero.	• Steals powers by murdering other Heroes and taking their brains.
• Wants to make the world a better place and to be part of something bigger than himself.	• Wants to be special and powerful, because he believes he and his family are insignificant.
• His mother thinks he is weak and incompetent, and wants him to be ambitious and ruthless, like the rest of the family.	• His mother thinks he's too "special" to be just a watchmaker, and wants him to have an important and lucrative job.
• Has no interest in power over anyone, though he's now the most powerful person on Earth.	• Becomes obsessed with power so he can control his own life and everyone around him.
• Will die to save a stranger, or to save the world; has never killed anyone.	• Will kill anyone who has a power, and anyone who gets in his way, including his own mother.

Gabriel Gray seems to have died with his mother. After her murder, Sylar never again shows guilt or remorse for any crime. The man who only a few hours earlier was terrified that he might cause the deaths of millions of innocents now seeks out Ted Sprague and murders him for his radioactive power. Then he stares over the city, savoring the thought of the upcoming holocaust as he lights up his hands again and again and whispers, "Boom!"

Chapter 6: That Delicious Power

"How can you stop what's coming, when you don't know anything about power?"
– Vision Sylar to Peter, *Fallout*

Sylar's delight in the thought of going "boom" is not so much about destruction as it is about power. In his old life, he felt powerless. He tells Chandra that his father "didn't give him much choice" about becoming a watchmaker. And when it comes to his mother, he can't even win an argument over a tuna sandwich. When he

IF SYLAR CAN ONLY GET ENOUGH POWERS TO BECOME UNTOUCHABLE, UNBEATABLE, THEN NO ONE WILL BE ABLE TO HURT HIM. AND THE REST OF THE WORLD WILL NEVER BE SAFE AGAIN.

want, she gets so agitated that he ends up eating the sandwich just to calm her down. It's obviously an old dance of emotional manipulation, which she has always led.

So while specific powers may be fun to play with, power itself is what Sylar has always craved. Telekinesis is his favorite and most used power, because it operates most directly and visibly on other people and things. Telekinesis makes Sylar the puppet master, and his victims become helpless toys under his control. And that's what he's hungry for: control – of his own life and everything that comes near him.

The Sylar of *Five Years Gone* tells Claire that he thinks he has collected enough powers, once he has hers. He finally feels safe (or almost safe; he still plans to eliminate the "competition" – all other Heroes who might be a threat to him). But our Sylar is still far from that goal. He craves as many powers as he can collect. If he can only get enough powers to become untouchable, unbeatable, then no one will be able to hurt him, say no to him, or make him do anything he doesn't want to do. Then, and only then, might the watchmaker's son feel safe. And the rest of the world will never

CLAIRE AND PRESENT DANGER

AN INTERVIEW WITH HAYDEN PANETTIERE

Hayden Panettiere is only 18 years old, but she's already displayed her talents in over 40 films and TV shows, including *Robot Chicken*, *Bring It On: All or Nothing* (as another cheerleader), *Commander in Chief*, *Malcolm in the Middle*, *Ally McBeal*, *Tiger Cruise*, *The Affair of the Necklace*, *Remember the Titans*, and *A Bug's Life*. She has also done voices for video-games and, of course, plays the indestructible cheerleader Claire Bennet on *Heroes*.
The popular actress talks about her experiences on the show so far…

relate to it – there's this huge conflict, huge issues going on in everyone's lives, but they've got huge issues of their own too that are normal.

Did you have any interest in superhero stories before you got involved in *Heroes*?
No, actually. I mean, I've always been a fan of Spider-Man and Superman and Batman. I have an 11-year-old brother who's into all that, and I have a cousin who does comic book designs, and he's amazing, so I grew up with him having a huge collection of comic books and action figures.

When you auditioned for Claire, what did they tell you they were looking for, as far as what she was like?
Well, she was a normal teenage girl. She was a cheerleader. What makes her interesting is that she is a normal teenage girl going through normal teenage things, going through what every girl goes through in high school, but she has these powers that make it even harder to grow up – it makes it scary and of course she thinks something's wrong with her. And it's what every teenage girl can relate to – up to the fact of being able to heal herself (*laughs*). I describe it as tissue regeneration.

Did you ever give any thought to any other profession besides acting?
HAYDEN PANETTIERE: No, I've been acting since I was eight months old (*laughs*). I was on a soap opera [*One Life to Live*] when I was four. I love acting. It's something I grew up doing, but if I didn't like doing it, I definitely wouldn't be here. I just did it and it eventually got to a point where I couldn't see myself doing anything else.

Before *Heroes*, it doesn't seem as though you performed in many supernatural/science-fiction genre pieces.
Yeah. I think the thing about [*Heroes*] that's really good is that it's a happy balance of making it not cheesy. It's more about the evolution of man. It's more how man is evolving, as opposed to these random people who just have these superpowers. I think it's different [from other superhero stories], because it's a lot more [set] in reality, a very reality-based show. It's about human issues, which is, I think, partially why it's appealing to people. People can

SINGER/ SONGWRITER

In addition to being an actress, Hayden Panettiere is a singer/songwriter whose work has been heard on movie soundtracks, including those for *The Dust Factory*, *Ice Princess*, *Cinderella III: A Twist in Time*, and *Bridge to Terabithia*. Now she is working on an album. "It's going good," she says. "It's that struggle at the moment of when we get it out, having time to promote it with the show, so we're trying to work that all out. Hopefully it will come out soon."

Claire makes some discoveries about her powers in season two's *Lizards*

What's it like doing the scenes when Claire has been mutilated and hasn't recovered yet, like when she's on the autopsy table?

Oh, yeah. I had to go do body scanning afterwards and it took about five or six hours to

going to do when you first go on. You just cross your fingers and hope for the best, because you really don't know how something like that is going to be received by the audience. Now we know that people generally like it and it was received well. We know the characters and we know each other. This show is probably unlike any show that anyone shoots, because we shoot it like a movie, and it's like we're doing a full-length feature film every day. In that respect, my past feature film career has definitely prepared me for this. But there's no place I'd rather be. I love my cast, I love my crew.

How is Claire different in the second season than she was in the first season?

She is a young girl, she has this beautiful naïvety about her. I think she lost a lot of it since the first season. I think she really grew up. I definitely

was getting sick of crying. I don't know about anyone else who was watching the show, but I was tired of seeing her cry. If you don't have kids, or if you haven't noticed, teenagers are selfish – I will vouch for that. She wanted what any teenager would want. She wanted to be normal, she wanted to be popular, she wanted to date the quarterback of the football team. Over time, she realized that by dismissing her powers, she was risking a lot of people's lives, that there was so much more she could do if she just came to terms with that. So she evolved, she learned to stand on her own two feet and stick up for herself. Hopefully, she'll continue doing that. I think she's just constantly

> *"WHAT MAKES CLAIRE INTERESTING IS THAT SHE IS A NORMAL TEENAGE GIRL GOING THROUGH NORMAL TEENAGE THINGS – UP TO THE FACT OF BEING ABLE TO HEAL HERSELF!"*

put on. The [fake] blood would run down. Can you imagine what blood starts to look like on your body after 10-and-a-half hours?

Is part of the appeal of playing Claire doing some of your own stuntwork?

Yeah. Actually, a lot of the fire stuff [in the premiere episode], that was me. My cheerleading outfit was actually flame-retardant material, so it wouldn't catch on fire, and there were times when I had to put on long underwear underneath my outfit and [flame-retardant] socks when I had to go into the train.

How was going into the second season different than going into the first season?

You don't know how well the show is

THE SUPERPOWER QUESTION

The *Heroes* actors are probably asked what superpower they'd like to have more than any other question. But is there a superpower Hayden Panettiere thinks it would be *helpful* for her and other actors to have? "The ability to be invisible," she replies. "Because I think, obviously, we can blame most of [the bad stories about celebrities in the press] on the people who are doing bad things they're not supposed to be doing. But at the same time, when you've got cameras in your face all the time, it leaves you no room to mess up even slightly, and things get turned around on you. So if I could walk out my door or drive my car and not be followed by paparazzi, I'd be a very happy person."

> *"I THINK I'VE SOMETIMES BEEN TYPECAST BECAUSE I'M BLONDE. YOU DON'T GET TO PLAY VILLAINS IF YOU'RE BLONDE, UNLESS YOU'RE SHARON STONE."*

growing and changing and discovering new things about herself.

In season two, she's really looking to figure out more about her powers, more about what she can do, how far she can push it, what happens when she does it. There are still some unanswered questions for her about her ability, how far her pain tolerance can go, whether she can actually die if something happens. We saw Peter in the first season – he had a shard of glass in his head and not until we pulled it out did he come back to life. But the question is, how long could he survive with that piece of glass in his head before he couldn't regenerate anymore? So I think she's just really pushing to find answers – on that level, she's just trying to figure out who she is and what she's doing and what she wants to do with her life and her ability.

It's almost a metaphor [about] teenagers – they're always trying to push their parents away, they're constantly trying to test the limits of their freedom and how far they can push things. It's sort of the same thing with Claire, she's just doing it in a different way – it is to have her freedom, but not to go to the mall with her friends or go on vacations, it's more to learn about herself and this ability.

All teenagers will understand that one. But I think it will continue to be a battle for her until she's an adult, and even then, her dad's going to want to protect her.

Is it hard making someone so physically durable seem so emotionally vulnerable?
Well, she *is* vulnerable. That's the interesting thing about her, the fact that she's a physically indestructible girl, but she's not emotionally or mentally indestructible. And that vulnerability is what makes people like her. When you approach it as an actress, it's just like playing any other character – you know, are they vulnerable, are they mean, are they nice, are they disturbed or happy? You make her like a normal teenage girl, and I actually *am* a teenage girl. When I'm acting, I forget about [Claire's] abilities. She has no idea how to handle it – that's the honest truth – so neither do I.

Have you ever felt invulnerable in real life?
Yeah. When I was younger, I always had that thought in my head for some reason. I could never imagine dying. It was impossible for me to die when I was younger. I wasn't indestructible in a way that I could heal myself, but when you're younger, death

Claire with her uncle, Peter

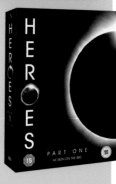

HEROES SEASON ONE DVDS

Prior to the *Heroes* Season One DVD set, Hayden Panettiere says she only remembers providing this kind of DVD commentary about her work on the ice-skating drama *Ice Princess*. She marvels at the wealth of material on the *Heroes* DVDs: "There are commentaries and there are about 50 deleted scenes, not outtakes, just scenes that were never used. It's incredible how many scenes you just forget are deleted. You're like, 'Oh, that's where that scene went!' It's really fun to watch because we really had limited time – it's only an hour-long show and you have such limited time to explain all this information that you need before you can get into the guts of the show. It really explains other characters, and goes more in-depth on other things that unfortunately [the show] didn't have time for."

What feature does Panettiere recommend viewers watch first on the discs? "It would depend on if they've seen the show or not. If they haven't, start with the [special edition] two-hour pilot. And then maybe the deleted scenes – I'm having fun watching the deleted scenes, but that's probably because I know what was deleted and what wasn't. And there are some goofy commentaries – I'm talking *goofy*. People will have fun with it."

Getting covered in blood is just part of the job for Claire...

FRIENDS
West, Zach,
Peter, The Haitian,
Meredith

ENEMIES
Lyle, Mr. Muggles,
Bob, Elle, Sylar

UNDECIDED
Mrs. Petrelli,
Nathan, HRG

isn't something that clicks in your head. Now it does, now I don't feel so indestructible – even though I'm playing someone indestructible.

Would you ever want to see Claire tip into 'the dark side'?
I wish I could – I'd turn bad in a second! I doubt it will happen, but in the show, anything is possible, so there's always that chance.

Why would you like to play a villain?
I think I've sometimes been typecast because I'm blonde. You don't get to play villains if you're blonde, unless you're Sharon Stone. It would just be exciting for me. People look at me as very sweet sometimes, and I would

never in a million years describe myself as sweet – never! I think it would be a blast. It's more fun to be bad – at least on the screen.

What are your fellow *Heroes* actors like?
Adrian [Pasdar], we've always said, is like the big brother. He always wants to take you here, take you there – he's the leader when [cast-members are on tour together]. Greg [Grunberg] is a goofball, Milo [Ventimiglia] is more of a flirt, Sendhil [Ramamurthy] and Masi [Oka] are great. Ali [Larter] and I are girls, we stick together. Jack Coleman I'm very close to. I get to work with him a lot, and he's so much fun. He's so

funny and he's such a bright man. It's fun to be around somebody like that who is bright, but funny at the same time. Zach [Quinto], who plays Sylar, is funny as anything, and he's a good friend, too. And Ashley Crow, who plays my mom – they all have their own personalities, and it's a hoot when we get together. Everyone has a crush on either Milo or Sendhil, but then I look at Greg and Adrian and Masi, and I see that everyone has crushes on them, too. We have a cast full of heartthrobs, what can I say?

It's not only a large cast, but it's a large cast of really good actors. When you're around such good actors, you want to bring yourself up

Claire with her adopted father, HRG

The Company's Bob captures Claire in season two

CLAIRE'S HERO-METER

We chart the highs and lows of Claire's heroic career

TOP

Using her power to allow her to get close enough to Ted to sedate him so he can't go nuclear.

Taking a bullet to gain Ted Sprague's trust in her, so she can free her family from a hostage situation.

MIDDLE

Claire tracks down her real mother, Meredith, despite HRG's attempts to keep them apart. She visits her, lying to both her parents.

Threatening Brody Michum with telling the world he attempted to rape her in an effort to protect other potential victims.

Punching Jackie the bitchy cheerleader for teasing Zach about his sexuality.

BOTTOM

When trying to protect her friend from the cheerleaders at her new school, she backs out at the last minute of doing a complicated gymnastic move in their trade-off.

She lets Jackie take the credit for saving the man in the train wreck.

to their level and strive to do your best. At the same time, in this show, we don't always get the chance to work with each other, so it's almost like showing off every time you get to work with [any cast-mate]. You're so excited, because it's like, "Ooh, I've got to be really good, because I'm working with so-and-so today."

What's it been like with the addition of new cast-members?

I haven't really gotten a chance to be around them a whole lot, other than a few cast [get-togethers] on set. But it seems everyone is pretty excited and thrilled to be a part of the show. It's an already-established show and it's been doing great and it's wonderful. Most of the people who have joined the cast have seen it and are just psyched to be here.

How do you feel about what's going on with Jack Coleman's Mr. Bennet this season?

Well, I think we all have proven in this show that [the characters] all have our dirty little secrets. I think him becoming the 'house dad,' the 'good dad,' wouldn't be very exciting. People like watching good-bad people, and you sometimes want to hate Jack's character and sometimes you love him. It's kind of a toss-up, depending on which side you're on. I think it's exciting for him – I'm excited to see what happens with *everyone*.

Do you find a lot of people you meet have a reaction to your portrayal of Claire?

Yeah. All the time – at the moment, I think it's meeting your peers [other actors who watch *Heroes*]. And you don't consider yourself one of the peers yet, because I've just gotten into it with the show and there are

"PEOPLE LOOK AT ME AS VERY SWEET SOMETIMES, AND I WOULD NEVER IN A MILLION YEARS DESCRIBE MYSELF AS SWEET – NEVER! IT'S MORE FUN TO BE BAD – AT LEAST ON THE SCREEN.

other people on the network who are huge stars and they know who you are and you're like, "Whoa! I'm used to watching you on TV, you're not supposed to know me."

How do you feel about the ardent fan reaction to Heroes?
It's very cool that they like it so much – it's like a pat on our backs every time they say something about it and love it. We're filming in the studio and it doesn't always click that 15 million people are watching the show, so it's cool to hear from them.

What can you tell us about the in-the-works Heroes video-game?
I don't know anything about the layout. I'm ecstatic. My cousin actually made me my first action figure – it's not 'real', obviously, but he did a really cool job. It's sitting on my shelf. It's always fun to see what they do with your characters [in terms of merchandising, comics, etc.] and in the video-game, to see what kind of animation they use. I would love to be involved with it. Other than that, I have no idea.

Is there anything else you'd like to say about Heroes?
I'm just really excited about it! ☼

HAYDEN PANETTIERE SELECTED CREDITS

FILM
Fireflies in the Garden (2006) – Young Jane Lawrence
Shanghai Kiss (2007) – Adelaide Bourbon
Bring It On: All or Nothing (2006) – Britney Allen
The Architect (2006) – Christina Waters
Mr. Gibb (2006) – Allyson "Ally" Palmer
Racing Stripes (2005) – Channing Walsh
Raising Helen (2004) – Audrey Davis
Remember the Titans (2000) – Sheryl Yoast
A Bug's Life (1998) – Dot

TV
Robot Chicken (2007) – Cheetara
Skater Boys (2006) – Kassidy Parker #2
Commander in Chief (2006) – Stacy
Law & Order: Special Victims Unit (2001-2005) – Angela Agnelli/Ashley Austin Black
Ally McBeal (2002) – Maddie Harrington
The Guiding Light (2000) – Elizabeth "Lizzy" Spaulding

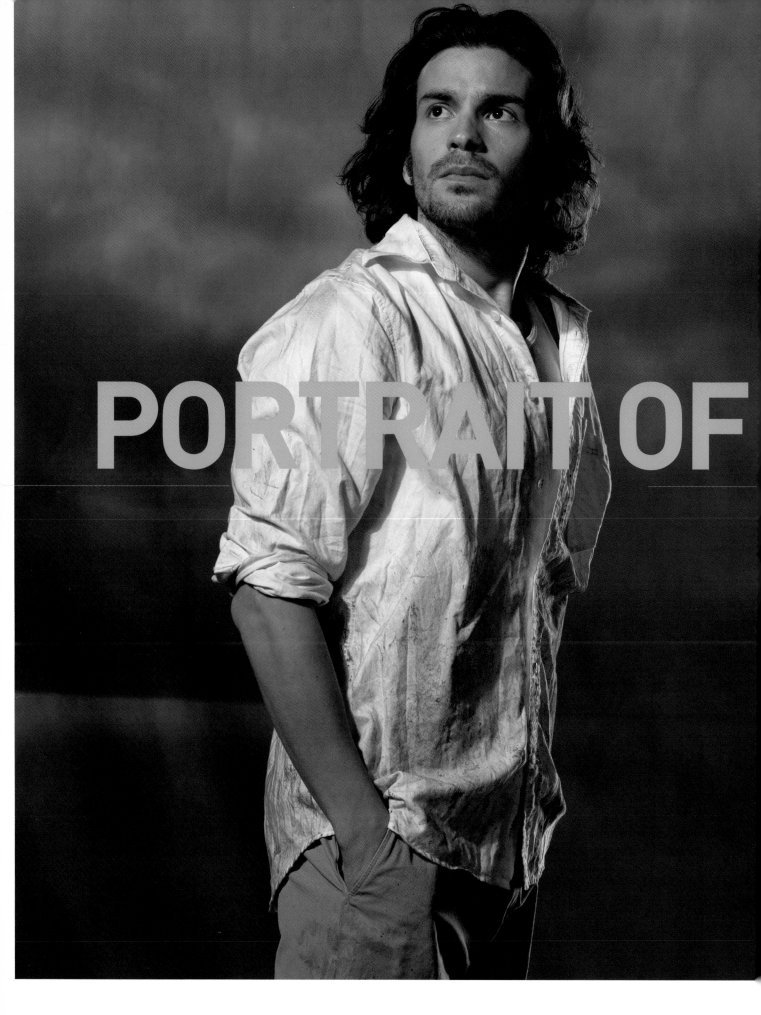

PORTRAIT OF

EACH HERO HAD AN IMPORTANT PART TO PLAY IN SEASON ONE, BUT ISAAC'S WAS ARGUABLY ONE OF THE MOST PIVOTAL. HIS PROPHETIC PAINTINGS HELPED SHAPE THE SHOW'S FIRST YEAR, AND HIS CHARACTER PROVIDED SOME OF ITS MOST DRAMATIC MOMENTS. ACTOR SANTIAGO CABRERA TALKS ABOUT HIS CHARACTER'S JOURNEY...

Heroes has many characters who are in emotional pain, but few have been as tormented as painter Isaac Mendez. Isaac had the power to paint the future, but at first believed he could only have visions when he was high on heroin. He managed to clean up, but the visions themselves were of terrible events, and his own life took an irreversibly tragic turn when he accidentally killed the love of his life, Simone Deveaux. By the time he was ultimately murdered by Sylar, Isaac was resigned to his fate.

characters with a lot of layers, and I just found that very intriguing. It was a small role in the pilot episode, but you could see that there were so many ways it could go.

Do you prefer playing Isaac when he's addicted, or when he's clean?
I just like the essence of who he is. He's

THE ARTIST

"I like the essence of who Isaac is. He's a tortured soul. He is who he is, so that tortured soul will be there regardless of if he's sober or if he's on drugs."

Santiago Cabrera, the actor who played Isaac, is considerably sunnier than his character. Born in Venezuela, Cabrera grew up in Chile and Canada, then had an acting career in Britain before moving to Los Angeles.

Cabrera's pre-Heroes credits include appearances on the BBC series Spooks (known as MI-5 in the US); the feature Haven with Orlando Bloom and Bill Paxton; a star turn as Emperor Octavius in the mini-series Empire; some on-screen Shakespeare as Lucentio in a reimagined The Taming of the Shrew; a lead in the romantic comedy Love and Other Disasters with Brittany Murphy, Gwyneth Paltrow, and Bloom again; and an appearance in the sports drama Goal II: Living the Dream. Since Heroes, Cabrera has completed filming the historical drama The Argentine, directed by Steven Soderbergh and starring Benicio Del Toro as Che Guevara.

How did you get into acting?
SANTIAGO CABRERA: I lived in many different countries. I was always very observant. I think that's what makes you [an actor].

What did you know about the character of Isaac when you first auditioned for Heroes?
The script was so different, it really caught my eye from the beginning. Isaac was described as a disturbed painter, a junkie, someone who's been going through a rough patch. I knew that he just painted this stuff and he discovered in the newspapers that [what he was painting] was happening and it was all freaking him out. So it was a pretty intense role – I thought he was one of these

a tortured soul, he's someone who's a complicated character. He is who he is, so that tortured soul that I'm talking about will be there regardless of if he's sober or if he's on drugs. So it doesn't make a difference for me – I'm really attracted to him as a person.

In the original unaired pilot, Isaac cut off one of his hands. How was that done?
I just had this green glove on [the hand that wasn't supposed to be there]. You remind yourself every time you look there that you don't have a hand, so it helps, and then they digitally remove it. It's this green glove and sometimes they give you tips like, "Don't put it there, put it there," because [if it's in the wrong place] it's harder for them to take it out when they do the effects afterwards.

Were you disappointed or relieved that Isaac was two-handed when Heroes went to series?

I think it didn't really make a difference in a way. I thought the hand thing was something that showed you, "Okay, this guy's intense and he's capable of being pretty crazy," but we didn't lose that, so it wasn't necessarily something that had to be given. It made things more practical for me – I didn't have to go around with a green glove and worry about where I placed my hand.

Did you learn anything about painting for the role?

Yeah, I did. I hadn't really done much painting before, but I loved it. You do a lot of things as an actor – you play different stuff and you try it all out. Painting is one of the first times I actually really [did] something that I think I would continue for myself. I am still painting. It's getting better, that's for sure.

Did you explore the world of comic books at all?

Because of the character, that's something else I've been doing – I've been getting more into the whole comics world. I've been reading a few comics and looking at Tim Sale's works – he's been doing my character's drawings. I met up with him before. He does *Daredevil* as well, and *Superman* – he does some very cool stuff. I was very impressed.

Do you feel *Heroes* resembles comic books in some ways?

There are a fair amount of similarities. I think it's something in between, in a way. At least in terms of my character, [comics have] been part of his background. Maybe as an artist, he's probably not been doing very well, but he's been making money and I think he's been working in comics for a while.

Did you do any research into addiction?

[Before being cast as Isaac], I hadn't really. I'd done it once for a play a long time ago, but still, that was in a different context. So I watched a lot of movies related to that and also looked into what people's direct experiences are, how they deal with it, what it does to you in your everyday life. I think the more you get into these things and the more you [learn], the more you start to relate to these people. So what's he doing every day, is he actually still craving, or is he not? Those things will dictate your actions afterwards.

I visited some rehabilitation centers and talked to people. I think the character would have gone through that a couple of times in his life and that's something that's been very helpful, and people have been very

Saving the World

Though he was often isolated and strung out in his loft, Isaac quickly became a pivotal character who tipped the balance of events in *Heroes*. We look at how Isaac related to the other *Heroes* characters...

Peter Petrelli
Though they were love rivals for Simone, Isaac was also the one who helped prove Peter's budding powers when Peter realized not only that Isaac had predicted the first time he flew, but that Peter had absorbed Isaac's power too.

Noah Bennet
Knowing Isaac's power, Mr. Bennet had him brought to The Company's hidden holding centre in Odessa, Texas and got him cleaned up.

Believing Isaac's power relied on him being high, Bennet ruthlessly ordered Eden to persuade him to start using again, all to keep his daughter safe.

Eden McCain
Eden's guilt over getting Isaac hooked on drugs again played a part in her trying to make Sylar kill himself. This inadvertently helped him to escape and sealed her own fate...

Simone Deveaux
Simone was in love with Isaac and desperately wanted to save him from his addiction. When she realized he didn't want her to help him however, she gave in to her attraction to Peter. When Peter turned up at Isaac's loft, Isaac tried to shoot Peter, and he accidentally shot her instead.

open and given me a lot to create details for it. I mean, getting into that world psychologically, as someone who is quite perturbed and has been going through a difficult time, the whole idea of why you get into drugs and where they take you and all that, is something I was always trying to get into his mind. It's exciting to get a role like this, because I think you just get to own it more and more as you go along. And I have created a lot of back-story for him myself, because there are a lot of things that aren't on the page that you need to figure out for yourself. I definitely did a lot of that.

Heroes is unusual in that, on some days, up to three episodes can be filming at once, with three different directors. Is that ever confusing?

It definitely makes it fun for me to watch. You kind of don't remember what you've read already and you forget other people's stories sometimes, because it gets mixed up with what's going on with what you're filming. I'm a huge fan of the show in that sense, so it's fun sometimes to be a bit lost with the whole thing. I mean, in terms of my character, I want to be solid with who he is and where he's at, so that's always clear for me, but it's fun to see the whole picture put together. It's a good experience as an actor, I think, because the directors work in such different ways that in a short amount of time, you get to experience

Santiago Cabrera Selected Credits

Despite only acting for a few years, Chilean-born Santiago Cabrera has already notched up a healthy list of credits. He's recently finished working on a Steven Soderbergh-helmed project, *The Argentine*, due for release this year. His acting work includes...

TV
Heroes – Isaac Mendez (2006-2007)
ShakespeaRe-Told – Lucentio (2005)
Empire – Octavius (2005)
As If – The Postman (2004)
Judge John Deed – Carlos Fedor (2003)
Spooks – Camilo Henriquez (2003)

MOVIES
Goal II: Living the Dream – Diego Rivera (2007)
Love and Other Disasters – Paolo Sarmiento (2006)
Haven – Gene (2004)

completely different methods of working and different approaches, so it makes you really open and receptive to what different people can do.

Did you expect *Heroes* to hit as big as it has?
I thought this show would make a difference, but I never thought it would be this big. Until you live it, you don't really know what it's like. It's been overwhelming in a certain way. The week with the Golden Globes – before, it was like, you go to work and you go home and your life doesn't really change too much. But now people are starting to recognize me more on the street. The reactions I get are all nice.

How was the reception at San Diego Comic-Con, before the show initially premiered on TV?
In a way, it was a reassurance of how "with it" people are, because that's the thing that impressed me the most. Maybe I wasn't so surprised, but what was really gratifying was how well people followed the show, because afterwards when they came up to us to ask things – they got all the nuances, all the little references, and they're really enjoying it and looking forward to the development of each character. And the fact that it's an ensemble cast means that different people have their favorites, so it's very good.

Is there any difference between acting in a fantasy series like *Heroes* and a more naturalistic drama?
The way *Heroes* is written is that every character is trying to deal with [the unusual events] in the way that real people would deal with it, so that's what I really like about it – that it's a drama with this extra element. I don't see it as being too "super," necessarily. I think people are pretty on top of what the theme of the show is and they're interested in the characters. And that's a nice thing to see, that all you guys are interested in these people and where they're going. ⤷

"Isaac was a small role in the pilot episode, but you could see that there were so many ways it could go."

Sylar
Knowing Isaac was on Chandra Suresh's list, Sylar coveted his power of prediction. Isaac's resulting murder was all the more horrifying because he saw it coming.

Mohinder Suresh
Taken to see Isaac by Peter to prove his power-absorbing ability, Mohinder was skeptical when he saw Isaac was a junkie. In the future world of *Five Years Gone* however, it's a page from the *9th Wonders!* comic book, drawn by Isaac, that convinces Future Mohinder to kill The Haitian instead of Hiro, allowing him to escape back to our time to prevent disaster.

Hiro Nakamura
Hiro realizes that Isaac's *9th Wonders!* comic book is predicting events in his own life, and tries to contact "Mr. Isaac". At first dismissive of the Japanese man on the phone, when the phrase "Save the cheerleader, save the world" matches what Peter says the Future Hiro told him, it sets in motion the Heroes' plan to save the world...

ON SALE

Think of *Heroes*, and several things spring to mind: Claire and her gross injuries. Sylar and his evil machinations. Peter's discovery of his various powers.... But one stand-out element is the prophetic artwork of Isaac, which is actually provided by hugely popular comic-book artist Tim Sale. Sale discusses his work, how he got the *Heroes* gig, and what his favorite pieces are…

On NBC's smash-hit show *Heroes*, it is life that truly imitates art. As a struggling artist and heroin addict, Isaac Mendez discovered he possessed the uncanny ability to glimpse into the future and paint prophetic visions while high on drugs. Over the episodes, those illustrations included anything from tender, quiet moments to horrifying murders and alarming apocalyptic disasters. But it wasn't actually the actor who played Isaac, Santiago Cabrera, who brought that precognitive gift to paper – it was in fact co-executive producer/writer Jeph Loeb's friend and frequent comic-book collaborator, Tim Sale, who constantly dazzled viewers with his poignant visuals, and whose art provided a fitting mood for the show.

"I got involved because Jeph gave me a call," Tim Sale recalls. "I have known Jeph for 20 years or so but he's known creator Tim Kring longer than that. I did not know Tim or his work, but they knew each other through Tim's first professional work in the movie industry, which was on *Teen Wolf Too*. So Jeph gave me a call and said, 'There is this guy, he has a hit show on NBC, *Crossing Jordan*, and he's written another script. He wants to make sure he can do all he can to sell the script to the powers that be.' Because there were comic-book overtones in the concept of the series and because Tim didn't know any artists, he called Jeph. Jeph suggested me, and one thing led to another."

Immediately, Sale was drawn into the entertaining world of these Heroes and their compelling individual journeys. "When I first read the script, in some ways it read like a Jeph Loeb comic-book script, which means I liked it," he grins. "In many other ways, it certainly seemed like a show I would want to watch – and it is."

A talented comic-book artist best known for *Batman: The Long Halloween* and *A Superman for all Seasons* (see boxout below), Sale's unique style proved to be an interesting fit for *Heroes*. "One of the funny things is I don't do likenesses very well," admits Sale. "That doesn't really seem to matter to the actors, who are naturally very protective of their likenesses and want to look the best they can. I've never had any of the actors ask if I can make them a little prettier. It is funny that doesn't turn out to be a big deal and that is also a part of why what I am able to do is important. For the most part, the stuff is on screen for a second or less so it needs to make an immediate impact, and comics is a great training ground for that sort of thing. My work is simple and not detail-oriented. Mine has fewer lines and is more expressionistic; there isn't an attempt to be realistic, so that lends itself to the immediacy of television."

TIM'S TITLES
A look at Tim Sale's comic-book work

Award-winning comic-book artist Tim Sale studied at the New York School of Visual Arts. Some of his earliest comics work was in 1983, in the series *Myth Adventures*. After this, Sale became primarily known for his collaborations with Jeph Loeb on such DC series as *Superman For All Seasons*, *Batman: The Long Halloween*, and *Batman: Dark Victory*, and for Marvel's *Spider-Man: Blue*, *Daredevil: Yellow*, and *Hulk: Gray*. He has also provided striking comic covers for various series.

COLOR SCHEME

Except to his legions of devoted fans, one surprising fact about Tim Sale is that he is actually color-blind, yet somehow he still manages to mix the spectrum up on *Heroes*. "The Peter/Simone picture is actually the only thing I have put color down on," reveals Sale. "I knew the red of the umbrella was the only color that was going to be on that image. I happened to have the red ink, so I did it myself. The way I work in comics is the same for the show – some of the art in comics is black and white and gray. I use charcoal, ink, and pencil and then I scan it, and send it to my colorist Dave Stewart, whose job it is to interpret it in color. It can be printed on paper, or for *Heroes*, it is blown up a great deal on canvas. I have ultimate say on it, but I almost never have to do corrections."

"WHEN I FIRST READ THE HEROES SCRIPT, IT CERTAINLY SEEMED LIKE A SHOW I WOULD WANT TO WATCH – AND IT IS."

Although Isaac's depictions turned out to be a major motivational factor for many of the characters, often thrusting them in one direction, in the early days, the producers never gave Sale an indication of how paramount his contributions would be. "They didn't map it out for me," he explains. "I am not entirely sure how much they had in their heads, but my sense of it is that it evolved. There isn't really another show that has art as an integral part of the story and also driving the plot. I find it

hard to believe they had that mapped out since the beginning, but maybe they did. Certainly Isaac and the idea he was a junkie, scared by the fact that when he was high he painted the future and what he foretold – including the mushroom cloud over Manhattan – could potentially come to pass, was all there in the pilot episode. I don't know if it took off, but my impression was it did."

Considering Sale was more familiar with the comic-book pencil and ink process, shifting

PAINTING PETER

Sale's initial attempt at one of the regular cast-members was Peter taking flight. Although it struck a chord with the viewers, it did require some fine-tuning. "I happened to be a *Gilmore Girls* fan and so I knew Milo Ventimiglia a little bit from that," explains Sale. "I had met him once and I am flattered he likes the painting and that other people respond to it, but I don't think it looks that much like him. That is the only drawing I did that I had to redo about four times. They weren't entirely happy with it, but they also didn't know what they wanted when they started asking me. The first thing they told me is, 'here is this guy, he's confused, and he jumps off the roof.' Mostly, they knew they wanted an upshot of him leaping off the roof, that he was wearing a long coat, and that it should flap behind him and sort of look like a cape. But he was terrified when I initially drew him, and it ended up with this serene pose. They figured out a better idea. It is in fact one of my least favorite pictures from the series. It is funny that so many people respond to it, but there you go!"

gears for Isaac's paintings wasn't that tough for him. "It all seems very easy to me in many ways," confirms Sale. "Two of the best-known images from the first season were Peter and Simone under the red umbrella in the rain and Hiro versus the dinosaur. That was like a monster comic cover, and I always thought of the Peter/Simone piece as a classic Will Eisner image. But again, you are looking for the most immediate impact. There is no background for either of those things, but there is a lot of mood involved, which is critical and one of my strong suits. I never said, 'I can't do this because I only do comics.'"

No matter what the assignment or deadline, Sale quickly developed a routine for going from the written word to canvas. "Throughout the first season, I was sent scripts but never read them after the pilot episode," he explains. "As a fan of the show, I didn't want to know anything and I realized early on I didn't need to in order to do my job. I would then have a conversation about the art. On the pilot episode, I spoke with Gay Perello, and after that, it was Ross Anderson. I also had Chuck Kim, who was a further connection because he had been Jeph and my assistant editor in comics at one time. I talked to Ross and Gay, and sometimes they felt I needed to come to the office because the writer or director wanted to talk to me. There are certain ones that are

Previous spread, center: Isaac's painting predicts his own death. Left: A classic Hiro painting from the first season. Below: Isaac's painting showed that a cheerleader – and the world – needed saving. Overleaf, bottom: Peter was in store for some season one pain – which came true in the episode *Homecoming*

more into that part of it than others, but there are also many times when I don't have to do anything other than get a phone call or email, go back and forth with a few people, and say, 'What is the point of this drawing, emotionally? What are the details I need to know? What are people wearing? What time of day is it?' You are really not much more involved than that. It is fairly simple and straight-forward. The challenge often comes from the speed they need things. At the worst it ever was, I needed seven paintings in five days. That might be an exaggeration, but there were more paintings than days. Mostly it's, 'We need this by next Monday, but I won't be able to have the final answers to your questions until Friday night.' All of the season two paintings were done within a month of the

beginning of scripting because they were a sequence of paintings, as opposed to season one, where they were ongoing and hadn't been planned out."

Isaac, Sylar, and Peter all have the power to see the future, but not all of them have the same artistic approach. "Sylar is very distinct," agrees Sale. "In fact, they went to a different artist. Sylar only had one painting and they went to Alex Maleev, who is an established comic-book artist, but has a very different style. Jeph had told me that he told Alex, 'I want it to look like he's just taken acid. His brain is so crazy, so that is how it comes out.' Some of Peter's drawings have been in colored pencil, but that was me drawing in pencil and then Dave coloring it like colored pencil on the computer. The style is the same, with no conscious difference between Peter and Isaac except for the technique. I just figured Peter absorbed Isaac's power directly. They are both good-hearted people compared with Sylar, so his picture needed to look dramatically different."

Furthermore, since Isaac actor Santiago Cabrera had no previous art background, the actor modeled certain aspects of Isaac after Sale. "Santiago actually came out here to Pasadena," says Sale. "He was interested in that actor way of coming out to see where I work. He also ended up taking classes, doing some life

"ONE OF THE FUNNY THINGS IS I DON'T DO LIKENESSES VERY WELL, BUT I'VE NEVER HAD ANY OF THE ACTORS ASK IF I CAN MAKE IT A LITTLE PRETTIER. IT IS FUNNY THAT DOESN'T TURN OUT TO BE A BIG DEAL"

ARTIST REFERENCES

Will Eisner
Will Eisner helped shape the modern day comic with his groundbreaking work on *The Spirit* and his many influential graphic novels, such as *A Contract with God and Other Tenement Stories* and *Invisible People*. He died in 2006, aged 88, and his legacy continues in the annual Eisner Awards ceremony, for achievement in comics.

Alex Maleev
Bulgarian artist Alex Maleev is well known for his photo-realistic and grainy artwork, which really developed in his work with writer Brian Michael Bendis on *Daredevil*. His latest work has been on the four-part *Halo: Uprising* mini-series and his illustrations will soon be seen in the new *Spider-Woman* comic.

drawings, and trying to immerse himself in it as much as possible. So he came out to my studio and looked around, absorbed stuff, and I did a little drawing for him. It didn't quite work, because I wasn't painting, but was working on paper with ink. And when I was working with Gay Perello on the pilot episode, she and other people from the props department took photographs of my studio and used that to help design the set."

Arguably, Sale's contribution to *Heroes* hinged on Isaac, so when he received the breakdown for the painting revolving around the character's gruesome demise, Sale was understandably shocked by the development – and slightly concerned! "Isaac has actually died a number of times," notes Sale. "In the pilot script, before it had been accepted, Isaac had painted the mushroom cloud over Manhattan in his own blood. He needed to paint strongly enough that he cut his wrist. They took this out of the final script, but originally he cut his hand off because he had been chained up by Simone to the radiator. So he was dead in the corner with this huge blood-red painting, which was really cool. They knew they didn't want him to die, because they wanted art to continue to be a part of the plot. Then he dies later when his brain is

One of the more striking and ambitious paintings was a decimated New York which sprawled all over Isaac's studio floor. "I always forget that one. It isn't one of my favorites, but it resonates with a lot of people," offers Sale. "That was a little more involved. I did a black and white with no gray illustration of that. It was never a painting, except on the floor, and they knew they wanted it to be that big. The way the prop department solved that problem is they actually had large, moveable five feet by five feet interlocking hard rubber mats – like you have in a gym – and they recreated my drawing directly on that. It is not a print. They can move that around to different places if they

"THE CHALLENGE OFTEN COMES FROM THE SPEED THEY NEED THE ART. AT THE WORST IT EVER WAS, I NEEDED SEVEN PAINTINGS IN FIVE DAYS."

taken out. I felt at that point it had been established that just because he had painted it, it didn't mean it was necessarily going to come to pass, because of the time-travel aspects of the show. I know towards the end of season one, Jeph had assured me I would have a job in the next year. I asked him again after the season one finale, because then Peter was gone. He said, 'Don't worry...'

"I miss Isaac. Santiago is a great guy and I liked having the character around. I don't really think they knew what to do with him other than that he was the guy who did the art. If we have another guy who does the art, we don't need to have him."

FAVORITE PAINTINGS

With over 40 art-pieces featured on *Heroes*, Sale has no problems singling out which ones were his stand-outs. "I have half a dozen," he says. "Other people would pick the red umbrella, Hiro versus the dinosaur, or the cheerleader menaced by the shadow on the steps. I actually like one that has very little screen-time, which is Suresh in the water spreading his father's ashes. That was an emotional one to do. I like both of the *9th Wonders* monster covers. There is one of Niki and Jessica reflected in the closed doors of an elevator. Niki is on one side and Jessica is on the other side. That was a lot of fun."

> "I MISS ISAAC. SANTIAGO IS A GREAT GUY AND I LIKED HAVING THE CHARACTER AROUND."

need to. It is a reinterpretation of my artwork, while all the others are prints. That was for practical reasons."

Debuting in 2006, Sale now has a season and a half of *Heroes*, not to mention a *TV Guide* cover of Sylar, Maya, Monica, and Micah under his belt. Naturally, he has hit his groove with some of the characters, while others continue to cause him trouble. "The primary challenge for me is how to get a good likeness," states Sale. "The drama and composition are challenges that are more comfortable for me, but the likenesses are always like, 'What am I going to do?' *TV Guide* was a very different thing. That is like doing a comic-book – it's not just flashed on the screen for a short period of time; people are holding it in their hands going, 'That doesn't look like Sylar!' In that regard, I like to draw the people I more consistently get a likeness for. I would say those characters are Sylar, because Zachary [Quinto] is practically a comic-book character, particularly with the long face, which is half-shaven and with big, dark eyebrows. HRG is perhaps my favorite character on the show, and Jack Coleman is a great guy. It is nice to have the glasses as a prop too, and Zach's eyebrows are almost the same thing. It's a hook; you almost don't have to draw the rest of the face and people will still know who you

are doing. As beautiful as Hayden Panettiere and Ali Larter are, there are no really distinctive hooks for me, so they are harder. Peter has now cut his hair, so I have no idea what to do! Hiro is a lot of fun."

With a successful career spanning over 20 years, Sale has put his signature stamp on the comic-book industry, but *Heroes* has opened up the flood-gates in terms of global recognition. "My credits in comics are prominent, but it is a much smaller world than the people who watch TV," he concludes. "I have a website and every day I get people asking where they can buy prints or get artwork. You actually can't, but these people only know me through *Heroes*, which I am extremely grateful for."

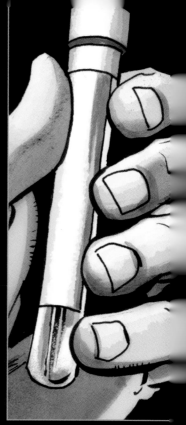

EIGHT WONDERS

A look at Isaac Mendez' "Series of Eight" paintings from season two

While prophetic artist Isaac Mendez fell victim to Sylar's torturous murder methods towards the end of season one, his future-predicting paintings still played a pivotal role in the show's second season. Mendez' grizzly on-screen death may have spelled the end for the ex-drug addict, but thanks to a series of eight paintings – stored in a Ukrainian warehouse and uncovered by Noah Bennet – we were treated, yet again, to the dynamic work of Tim Sale – the man behind Mendez' paintbrush. Here, we take a look at those paintings, and their significance on the show...

#1

THE IMAGE: A MAN LYING IN A POOL OF BLOOD.
FIRST APPEARANCE: *LIZARDS* (S2, EP2)
SIGNIFICANCE: THIS PAINTING DEPICTS THE DEAD BODY OF KAITO NAKAMURA AFTER HE HAS BEEN MURDERED – THROWN FROM THE TOP OF ISAAC MENDEZ' BUILDING BY ADAM MONROE.
EVENT OCCURRENCE: *FOUR MONTHS LATER...* (S2, EP1)

1/8

#2

THE IMAGE: A YOUNG WOMAN LYING ON SOME STEPS – PRESUMABLY DEAD.
FIRST APPEARANCE: *THE LINE* (S2, EP6)
SIGNIFICANCE: THIS IS CLAIRE BENNET AFTER SHE HAS BEEN DROPPED
FROM A GREAT HEIGHT BY HER BOYFRIEND, WEST – A PRANK TO UNSETTLE
BITCHY CHEERLEADER DEBBIE.
EVENT OCCURRENCE: *THE LINE* (S2, EP6)

#3

THE IMAGE: A CLOSE-UP OF SOMEONE
HOLDING A TEST TUBE.
FIRST APPEARANCE: *THE LINE* (S2, EP6)
SIGNIFICANCE: THIS IS A VARIANT OF
THE SHANTI VIRUS, WHICH PETER PETRELLI
IS HOLDING HERE. MOMENTS LATER,
HE DESTROYS IT.
EVENT OCCURRENCE: *POWERLESS* (S2, EP11)

3/8

#4

THE IMAGE: A WOMAN
POUNDING ON A DOOR.
FIRST APPEARANCE:
THE LINE (S2, EP6)
SIGNIFICANCE: THIS IS
NIKI/JESSICA SANDERS
BEING CONTROLLED
BY MAURY PARKMAN,
AS SHE TRIES TO
BREAK INTO BOB'S
OFFICE TO ATTACK HIM.
EVENT OCCURRENCE:
OUT OF TIME (S2, EP7)

4/8

#5

THE IMAGE: A MAN LOOKING ON IN HORROR AT SOME KIND OF BIOHAZARDOUS DISASTER.
FIRST APPEARANCE: *THE LINE* (S2, EP6)
SIGNIFICANCE: THIS PAINTING DEPICTS PETER PETRELLI IN AN ALTERNATE FUTURE, AS HE WITNESSES THE DEVASTATING EFFECTS OF THE SHANTI VIRUS ON NEW YORK CITY.
EVENT OCCURRENCE: *OUT OF TIME* (S2, EP7)

5/8

6/8

#6

THE IMAGE: TWO MEN SWORD-FIGHTING.
FIRST APPEARANCE: *THE LINE* (S2, EP6)
SIGNIFICANCE: THIS PAINTING CAPTURES FORMER FRIENDS HIRO NAKAMURA AND TAKEZO KENSEI BATTLING IN 17TH-CENTURY JAPAN.
EVENT OCCURRENCE: *OUT OF TIME* (S2, EP7)

7/8

#7

THE IMAGE: A MAN HOLDING A SMOKING GUN, TEARS IN HIS EYES.
FIRST APPEARANCE: *THE LINE* (S2, EP6)
SIGNIFICANCE: THE MAN IN THIS PAINTING IS MOHINDER SURESH, WHO IS FORCED TO FIGHT
NOAH BENNET SO THAT HE CAN GET TO CLAIRE AND HER HEALING BLOOD.
EVENT OCCURRENCE: *CAUTIONARY TALES* (S2, EP9)

THE IMAGE: A MAN IN THE FOREGROUND WITH A BULLET HOLE IN HIS EYE, AS A COUPLE SEEMINGLY EMBRACE IN THE BACKGROUND.
FIRST APPEARANCE: *KINDRED* (S2, EP3)
SIGNIFICANCE: DURING A FACE-OFF BETWEEN NOAH BENNET AND THE COMPANY'S BOB AND ELLE, BENNET GOES TO SHOOT BOB, BUT HE IS SHOT IN THE EYE BY MOHINDER SURESH. WEST CONSOLES CLAIRE IN THE BACKGROUND, BEFORE THEY PRESUMABLY FLY OFF AND ESCAPE.
EVENT OCCURRENCE: *CAUTIONARY TALES* (S2, EP9)

#8

8/8

SPLIT PERSONALITY
ALI LARTER

Arggh! Did Niki Sanders really die in that explosion in the season two finale? True to *Heroes* form, even if actress Ali Larter knows, she can't and won't tell us! Here's what the actress from New Jersey – who had four feature films out in 2007 (the sci-fi action thriller *Resident Evil: Extinction*, the music drama *Crazy*, the Indian musical comedy *Marigold*, and the National Lampoon farce *Homo Erectus*) – can say about *Heroes* and her super-strong, multi-persona character.

When Larter first read for *Heroes*, she had recently moved to Los Angeles from New York. "The key is really about looking for challenging material. And this [was the first time] I decided to read pilots. Most of them I thought were okay, but really didn't have a character where I felt like, if this show did go for six years, I could really grow and live with. And when I read Tim Kring's [*Heroes*] pilot, I was totally blown away, because I haven't gotten many chances in my career to really deal with complex women, and Niki is complex, to say the least," Larter laughs. "She allows me to internalize what's happening and really goes through thought processes of what's happening in her life. It's not all on the page, it's not just hand-fed to you. So I was blown away by his writing and his ideas and kind of the themes in the show."

Larter says she didn't fully understand Niki's motives before making the pilot. "David Semel is such an extraordinary director, and one of the things that we talked about – because I didn't have any answers when I was shooting the pilot, it was just more like questioning what was happening – was, what is going on? Is this a survivalist who's trying to protect her son? For me, it was just a form of anxiety [as Niki]. [Another reason] I was attracted to playing this is, we don't all of a sudden know what our powers are. So it's all internalized. And [the super-powered characters] are trying to get their kids to school, and we're trying to deal with all these things that are happening in our lives while this is growing inside us. That exploration is really interesting."

With a laugh, Larter notes that she did a little computer exploration into Niki's first-season career as an online fantasy provider. "I did pop online a little bit and watched some of that to get an idea of it, and it's such a fresh concept! I mean, let's be honest, I haven't actually seen it anywhere [on TV] and I think more people do it than like to talk about it. It's such a strange kind of culture. You watch these people and they're so disconnected. I mean, there's no physical intimacy, but they're able to live any persona that they want to live. So I thought it was interesting from a psychological point of view. I think all the girls [who have similar jobs] are acting. I don't think they're there because they want to be."

As far as *Heroes*' depiction of Niki's profession, Larter says, "I think they shot it so well and did it so tastefully. She's a webcam stripper. At some point, she needs to use this at this point in her life to pay her bills and get by the way that she can. So for me, that's her act of desperation. So you need to understand what this woman's willing to do and how her world's crumbling

"WHEREVER THE *HEROES* WRITERS TAKE ME WITH THIS, I'M UP AND READY FOR IT. I'M SURROUNDED BY SUCH A TALENTED TEAM OF WRITERS."

Left: Jessica takes over; This pic: Future Niki and Future Hiro

Left: Niki tries to figure her strange powers out in season one.
Above: Niki with her son Micah

around her, and she's doing whatever she can just to get by. Some people go right and some people go left – I don't know if she always makes the right decisions, but she just kind of does the best that she can. Those are things that are interesting as a character, and one of the reasons I signed on to the show was the question of what led her to get there? What happened in her life to get her to a place that she'd be willing to do that? That stuff doesn't scare me – for me it's just about understanding why she does the things that she does. The way that Tim [Kring] wrote it opens up 100 avenues of understanding where she is, and just with what's on the page, he really built an interesting woman."

Not that it's been a breeze. Scenes where Larter switched, without the mirror, between Niki and Jessica were at first, she says, "Really difficult. A lot of [the performance] is in the physicality for me, but my first reaction when I saw [the script] was, 'No, I can't do this.' I was stricken with fear. The truth is, on this show, we're so pushed creatively – if by chance it doesn't work, it's not going to

"MY FIRST REACTION WHEN I SAW THE SCRIPT WAS, 'NO, I CAN'T DO THIS.' I WAS STRICKEN WITH FEAR..."

make it on the air. So for me, that really gave me freedom as an actor to go for it 100 percent. We did rehearsals and we're all really lucky to have great camera guys visually [telling] the story. I separate the characters. They're two different people to me, and I really worked on it and then you've got to just let it fly."

Niki started season two without her homicidal alter-ego Jessica. "Unification happened," Larter explains. "I think the writers looked at [the first season] and really saw what worked and what didn't, and what happened for the second

season was, they tightened it up, really focused on the things that work. I'm really excited to be a part of that."

What have the changes meant for Niki? "She's almost going through what most characters went through in the first season – understanding, discovery – it got very, very complicated with Niki."

Series creator Tim Kring and his staff come in for high praise from Larter. "Wherever they take me with this, I'm up and ready for it. I'm surrounded by such a talented team of writers, and Tim comes from *Crossing Jordan*, and he must have kept this secret [of wanting to do sci-fi/fantasy] inside of him for so long, because it's such a departure from the last show. I just feel totally protected and excited with wherever he's taking me and my character."

Heroes' storytelling style, with different episodes emphasizing different characters, appeals to Larter as both a viewer and an actress. "I think it's one of the things that keeps it fresh. We [the actors] aren't [working] five days a week, 16 hours a day, so we get a chance to actually develop our characters, do research, and I think it's what keeps the show really creative and it's what keeps people coming back for more, too."

How does the physicality on *Heroes* compare to Larter's strenuous action-hero work on *Resident Evil: Extinction*? "I would say it's as physical. *Resident Evil* got really intense because of the heat – 120 degrees down in Mexico, and we were just sweating. It was so warm, people were dropping like flies. So that was definitely the hard part, the weather."

Are there stunts on *Heroes* that Larter views with particular pride? "I thought that the final season one battle was pretty cool – the fighting and the camera going around."

Working on sci-fi/fantasy projects has considerably increased Larter's appreciation for the genre. "I didn't really understand this genre as much when I was younger, when I first started in this business, and now I'm so much more into the fantasy idea. It's like when you're a little kid and you're able to dream these things, and it's on the screen. I'm much more into it than I've ever been before."

Whether or not Niki comes back from the burning building, Larter says she's been having a blast on *Heroes*. "After reading what Tim wrote for the pilot, I felt like [I could have] years to live with her. It's not like I'm playing a lawyer on some drama and giving banter back and forth. So if it does get to go that long – incredible. As long as it's great material and everyone is really there, wanting to be there and wanting to do their best work, I'll be so happy to be part of it." ⟲

ALI LARTER SELECTED CREDITS

TV
Dawson's Creek (1998) – Kirsty Livingstone
Just Shoot Me (1998) – Karey Burke
Chicago Hope (1998) – Samantha
Suddenly Susan (1997) – Maddie

FILM
Crazy (2007) – Evelyn Garland
Resident Evil: Extinction (2007) – Claire Redfield
A Lot Like Love (2005) – Gina
Final Destination 2 (2003) – Clear Rivers
Jay and Silent Bob Strike Back (2001) – Chrissy
Legally Blonde (2001) – Brooke Taylor Windham
Final Destination (2000) – Clear Rivers
Drive Me Crazy (1999) – Dulcie
Varsity Blues (1999) – Darcy Sears

Niki/Jessica and D.L. come face to face with Mr. Linderman

> "FROM THE MOMENT I READ THE FIRST SCRIPT, I REALLY DID THINK *HEROES* WAS SOMETHING SPECIAL."

THE
UNTOUCHABLE

LEONARD ROBERTS

Leonard Roberts' *Heroes* character D.L. Hawkins started out a little on the worrying side – he'd walked out of jail after he discovered he could pass through solid matter – but he proved himself the model of a loving husband to Ali Larter's Niki and devoted father to Noah Gray-Cabey's Micah. Series creator Tim Kring says this was the whole point. "When Leonard comes on and he's got this very soulful quality to him, it undercut the expectation of who that character was." Since D.L.'s tragic death, shown in the episode *Four Months Ago*, Roberts has filmed a lead role in the upcoming horror film *The Stone House* and hasn't left his *Heroes* colleagues behind – as of this writing, he's on stage in Los Angeles at the Geffen Playhouse in the Civil

Leonard as D.L. with screen wife
Niki, played by Ali Larter

War musical *Atlanta*, co-written and co-directed by Adrian Pasdar (who plays Nathan Petrelli).

What was Roberts' first impression of D.L.? "Well, it was laid out in the script. There was a lot to glean from what was already written. You knew that the guy had a serious physical presence, and I think one of the first descriptions of him in the script was, 'Mean as hell.' And so you think, what makes somebody mean, and what gets them to this place where they are when they're introduced, and I just tried to think about what I had to bring to that. One of the first things that really caught my attention was his connection to his son and the pain that comes out of the inability to [take care of] someone you love. And I thought, 'That's what I'm going to hold onto, that's what I'm going to go in with and let that be the fuel for making me mean.' If you were taken away from someone that you cared about and felt ineffectual in your life, that would make you unhappy. There's a sense that violence is a part of this guy's life."

D.L. was originally in the pilot, but not the one that aired on NBC. Roberts explains, "There was a change with the characters. I had all the faith in the world in Tim and his crew, and I knew what was coming down the pike. I was really excited – I think it was a challenge as an actor to have these preconceived ideas, because Niki is laying out to Micah and the cops who D.L. is, and when he shows up, it kind of turns that on its ear. I looked forward to

it and it was fun to sit back and watch it. I was a fan from the beginning – I'm calling my [*Heroes* cast-mates] up, saying 'Man, you rocked in that scene'!"

What does Roberts think D.L. feels when he passes through matter? "I think it depends on where he's at. In the beginning, there could have been some sensation of something on the molecular level between him and the object. In time, he got used to it, but in moments where physically he's down, maybe it's like a tactile reminder of, this is still outside of him."

How are those scenes filmed? "We do a lot of green-screen," Roberts says. "We'll establish the 'before' [the area before D.L. passes through it] and then we take [the set piece] out and then I do my thing, whatever it may be, and then we add it again, and they just put it all together [in editing]."

Once D.L. reconnected with Niki and Micah, how did Roberts find playing the husband and father aspects of the role? "I think there's just something that's so organic and so great about it – it's funny. Niki and D.L., their connection is [sometimes] tenuous, but the thing that brings them together is their undying love for this boy and I just loved being a part of that. The fact that Noah is a genius makes it a lot easier – he's such a professional. I feel sometimes like I'm the kid, but he's fantastic. I love him. Ali's the consummate perfectionist. She's there to play, and that's good. I come from the stage, so

Leonard as D.L. with screen son Micah

it's not fun unless we're playing. It's always a volley. Whatever she's giving me is what I'm going to react to. When we get into a room, we're not leaving until it's right, so it's fun to be [working with] that."

Like other actors who have scenes with Masi Oka's time-freezing Hiro, Roberts had to stay perfectly still in a shot – that also required him to be near a burning car holding a woman in his arms. "It actually wasn't as complicated as it may have seemed," Roberts relates. "Early in the morning, we got there, we did the first part, the approach up to the car, and then we blew it up, and then Mark Kopak, our VFX guy, came in, and we set up all the stuff for Masi to freeze time and they just put it all together." The tough part? "How long can you freeze?" Roberts laughs. "On that particular day, it was intense, because I was holding a woman at an angle, so I had her weight, and I'm just like trying to keep it still, but it can be a challenge. And then I got into it. I was, 'Let's make it look more like it was in motion.' For that to be the case, we've

got to bend more and we've got to make it awkward, to really give the effect that time stopped. So it was fun."

The willingness of various characters to test their abilities against things like blazing vehicles, that show of faith, is something Roberts loves about *Heroes*. "Yeah, go big or go home. That's one of the things I was really drawn to is that with faith, you don't take a small step. Faith is about a big step."

How did Roberts find the fan reaction to *Heroes* when the cast appeared at Comic-Con 2006? "It was great. It wasn't nearly as fanatical as I thought it was going to be. Everyone was so with-it and so intelligent with questions and responses, and they were so passionate about it. These people so respect the genre and I think they respect what Tim is trying to do, to make a show that is not necessarily a genre show, but employs some of these genre ideas around a character-oriented show."

When he first became involved with the series, did Roberts expect *Heroes* to become the phenomenon it is now? "It was always my hope," he says. "From the first page, I really did think it was something special, and I just wanted to be a part of it once it became a possibility. I just wanted it out there so bad, I wanted to be on board."

THE I.T. BOY

NOAH GRAY-CABEY

At age 12, Noah Gray-Cabey is already a veteran of series television, having been a regular on *My Wife and Kids* for two years, as well as a guest on *CSI: Miami*, *Grey's Anatomy*, and *Ghost Whisperer*, with a role in the feature *Lady in the Water* thrown in for good measure.

The young Newry, Maine native says he didn't know much about his character, Micah Sanders, when he initially auditioned for *Heroes*. "I got the little thing that comes with the audition and it said [Micah is] a smart kid, but he only has his mom right now, so I was pretty excited – it sounded like a pretty dramatic role. This is the most dramatic role I've ever had, so I'm really excited about seeing how far I can go with my acting abilities and maybe see if I can learn something new from the other great actors on the show."

Micah uses his technology-manipulating gift

MUM'S THE WORD
Ali Larter discusses playing Micah's mom

One thing that hasn't changed over the course of *Heroes* is Ali Larter's enjoyment of playing mother to Noah Gray-Cabey's Micah. "Working with Noah is incredible. He's such a talented guy. He's smart, he's giving, he's a little genius." It's not all that different from acting opposite an adult, except, Larter observes, "I have to watch my language when I'm on set," she laughs. "He's just a sweetheart and he's a really great actor. Even though I don't have any children, I'm very close with my nephews and I watch my sister with her children, and it's such an incredibly powerful bond, so for me, it's just about exploring that."

Niki and Micah by D.L.'s grave-side

"THIS IS THE MOST DRAMATIC ROLE I'VE EVER HAD, SO I'M REALLY EXCITED."

Gray-Cabey gives an example. "Ali [Larter, who plays Micah's mother Niki] has really helped me a lot. I had this crying scene to do in [the first season], and she made it possible for me to do it. I could not have done it [otherwise], so it was really nice that she was able to do that for me."

For a long time, Micah's loyalties were divided between his parents – the character would sometimes disobey his father D.L. to contact his mother, even when the schizophrenic Niki-as-Jessica was trying to kill her erstwhile mate. "I think Micah felt bad," Gray-Cabey explains. "I think he felt like his mom

needed him. That's what Jessica said to him, so he felt pressure to go and tell his mom."

What's it like playing a character with conflicting allegiances? "It's fun and difficult. It's challenging – but it's fun to have a challenge. I'm very excited."

Even after beginning work on *Heroes*, Micah's powers came as a surprise to Gray-Cabey. "I obviously thought this is an awesome show. When I read that script with me fixing the dead payphone, I was like, 'Whoo, yay!' I was going, 'I wonder what that means for the character.' I was very curious – I'm still curious."

NOAH GRAY-CABEY SELECTED CREDITS

TV
Ghost Whisperer (2006) – Jameel Fisher
Grey's Anatomy (2006) – Shawn Beglight
My Wife and Kids (2002-2005) – Franklin Aloysius Mumford
CSI: Miami (2004) – Stevie Valdez

FILM
Lady in the Water (2006) – Joey Dury

Sign of the Times

Examining the *Heroes* Helix

Heroes has provided us with plenty of mysteries over its first two seasons. One of the biggest has been the frequent appearances of the strange Helix symbol – it just seems to crop up everywhere, from feudal Japan to contemporary New York. Here we take a look at where this enigmatic sign has appeared and what it could possibly mean for our Heroes...

It's not just their abilities that set the Heroes apart from the rest of society – their differences are also highlighted by the mysterious Helix symbol that seems to follow them wherever they go.

If you've watched *Heroes* for more than five minutes (and if you're reading this, we'd imagine you've watched it far more than that!), you've no doubt noticed the symbol – whether it's as Jessica's tattoo or as the emblem on the hilt of Hiro's sword. But what does the symbol mean? And why is it so common in the *Heroes* universe? To find the answers would require the obsessive curiosity of Mohinder Suresh, examining the evidence, and coming up with plausible conclusions. Nearly every character in the show has encountered the symbol in one form or another, even if they weren't aware of it at the time, and each encounter tells viewers and fans a little more about what the Helix could mean...

LOCATING THE SYMBOL

The Helix symbol crops up even more often than you may realize. Let's take a look at some of its appearances...

• On the cover of the Isaac Mendez-drawn comic book *9th Wonders!*, where Hiro cheers his teleportation to New York. "Yatta!" (*Don't Look Back*) (see pic 1)

• On the map in Chandra Suresh's apartment. (Various episodes) (2)

• On the sketch Peter draws in hospital. (*Don't Look Back*) (3)

• In between the lines of code in Chandra Suresh's computer program list. (*Don't Look Back*) (4)

• In a crime scene swimming pool that Matt Parkman investigates. (*Don't Look Back*) (5)

• On the cover of the popular book about genetics and superhuman abilities, *Activating Evolution*, by Chandra Suresh. (Various episodes) (6)

• On the side of Claire's geometry textbook. (*One Giant Leap*) (7)

• Drawn all over the photos and newspaper clippings on the map in Sylar's apartment. (*One Giant Leap*)

• As necklace pendants worn by both The Haitian and Peter Petrelli. (Various episodes) (8)

• On the hilt of Hiro's Takezo Kensei sword (and on the toy replica of the sword Hiro plays with as a boy) (Various episodes) (9)

• As a tattoo on Jessica's shoulder (though not her alter ego Niki's) and on Peter's arm in season two. (Various episodes)

• On various notes left on computers and desks relating to people with special abilities. (Several episodes)

• As graffiti in a Utah bus stop where Micah waits. (*Homecoming*) (10)

• In Chandra Suresh's lizard tank. (*Godsend*) (11)

• In a plate of pasta eaten at an Italian restaurant (where Claude swipes a cellphone). (*Godsend*) (12)

• Throughout the offices of the Primatech Paper company. (Various episodes)

• Within the Petrelli Law offices and Primatech Paper logos. (Various episodes)

• On the door to the Bennets' home, where Ted Sprague goes nuclear. (*Company Man*) (13)

• On the floor of Chandra Suresh's apartment, made up of the wooden remains of a smashed bookcase, following a fight between Sylar and Peter Petrelli. (.07%) (14)

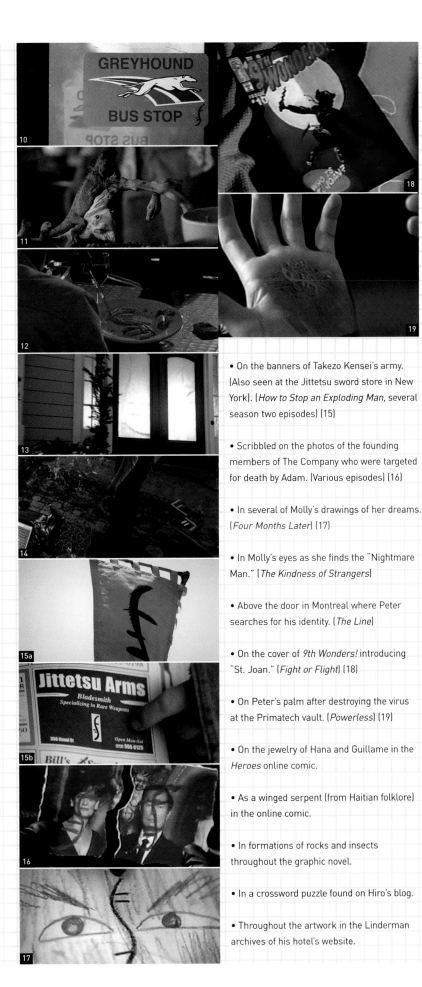

- On the banners of Takezo Kensei's army. (Also seen at the Jittetsu sword store in New York). (*How to Stop an Exploding Man*, several season two episodes) (15)

- Scribbled on the photos of the founding members of The Company who were targeted for death by Adam. (Various episodes) (16)

- In several of Molly's drawings of her dreams. (*Four Months Later*) (17)

- In Molly's eyes as she finds the "Nightmare Man." (*The Kindness of Strangers*)

- Above the door in Montreal where Peter searches for his identity. (*The Line*)

- On the cover of *9th Wonders!* introducing "St. Joan." (*Fight or Flight*) (18)

- On Peter's palm after destroying the virus at the Primatech vault. (*Powerless*) (19)

- On the jewelry of Hana and Guillame in the *Heroes* online comic.

- As a winged serpent (from Haitian folklore) in the online comic.

- In formations of rocks and insects throughout the graphic novel.

- In a crossword puzzle found on Hiro's blog.

- Throughout the artwork in the Linderman archives of his hotel's website.

INTERPRETING THE SYMBOL...

A Godsend?

Taking into account its many diverse appearances, giving an overall interpretation of the Helix is problematic.

Ando described it literally as the combination of two Japanese characters – the characters for *sai* (which means "great talent; genius; wisdom of the ancients") and *yo* (which means "godsend; bestowing of great ability; providing or imparting talent"). Both seem suited to describe someone with Hero powers.

It's logical to assume that Takezo Kensei/Adam Monroe first used the symbol as the combination of the two Japanese characters, taking it on as the symbol of his personal army, and his own family crest. Ando and Hiro have both stated that the symbol means "godsend" and was Kensei's logo. But is that the sole meaning or interpretation of the symbol? Why did Kensei create it? The answers to those questions may be found in the work of Dr. Chandra Suresh.

The Next Step in Human Evolution?

As demonstrated by the symbol's use on the cover of his book, scientist Chandra Suresh recognized its relationship to the people he was finding who had undergone some kind of genetic shift, and had obtained superhuman abilities. No doubt Suresh had encountered the

symbol while interviewing his subjects for his book. The Helix has manifested itself as a tattoo in some cases, for instance on Jessica Sanders and Peter Petrelli.

As a brilliant geneticist, Suresh had delved into the Human Genome Project. Strands of DNA and its companion RNA were at the forefront of his mind, since he dealt with them in his daily work. Coming across the symbol in his study of the superhuman, Chandra must have viewed it as half of a DNA or RNA strand. This is just as logical an interpretation of the symbol as the combination of the Japanese characters. After all, the genes of the superhuman subjects play an important part in the development of their powers.

The symbol represented the next step of human evolution to Chandra Suresh – but why this particular symbol? Why would the half-DNA/combined Japanese letters look so similar and show up in so many cultures? Why would people who lived centuries apart and across the world coincidentally find an identical symbol?

Genetic Recognition?

It is possible that both Kensei and Suresh interpreted and used the symbol in the way they did because of a deep-seated genetic recognition. Many scientists and philosophers believe that there are messages and symbols buried deep within human consciousness – even to the genetic level. It is possible that the symbol is just such a message, carried in the "genetic memory" of those who will undergo the mutation of their DNA that will allow them to obtain special powers, making them different to the majority of humanity. As access to these abilities is discovered, the genetic memory is triggered, and the superhuman among us are given a subconscious recognition of the symbol. Perhaps it was placed in the genetic memory of those with abilities to help them identify their unique powers, and begin using them. Could it be a message in a bottle from

Mother Nature sent to her future creations to help guide them as they grew and developed?

A Twist of Fate?

While the theory of genetic memory is feasible in light of the constant recognition of the symbol among those with superhuman abilities, it becomes problematic when one considers the large number of non-human manifestations of the symbol over the years.

Would nature cause clouds to form in the shape of the symbol to communicate with the genetically altered? Would cockroaches appear to run around like the symbol so a resident of an infected apartment would realize they have strange powers? Possibly. However, the appearance of the symbol in non-human, man-made, unnatural circumstances calls this theory into question. Certainly, the subtle placement of the symbol in the logos for Linderman's casino, Primatech Paper, Kensei's army, and the law offices of the Petrelli patriarch could be dismissed as being put there by those with the genetic memory of the symbol. But what about its showing up in between the letters and words of Chandra Suresh's computer program tracking those with powers? It seems unlikely that Chandra would take the time to type the words in such a way as to create the symbol. Even stranger is the appearance of the symbol in a plate of pasta and a lizard tank. These, as well as the computer program, may have been subconscious creations based on genetic memory, or maybe just a freak of probability.

Perhaps most mysterious is the appearance of the symbol in powder on Peter Petrelli's palm after he destroyed the virus Adam hoped to unleash on humanity. There was no manual creation of the symbol, nor genetic memory to explain its existence in this case. Regardless, somehow the symbol showed up, consistently linking it further to those with special powers.

Genetic Memory As Folklore?

Throughout the generations, folk tales from several different cultures have also interpreted the symbol. The primary example of this is, of course, in the tales of Takezo Kensei. Given the possible genetic memory that Kensei himself had, there's little wonder as to why the symbol showed up here.

Similarly, in modern folklore – that of comic books – the symbol's inclusion could be due to the genetic memories of the comic book creator, Isaac Mendez. However, in Haitian folklore, learned by The Haitian during his boyhood, a winged serpent learned to fly and formed the symbol with his body. This story could symbolize a human discovering his own ability to fly and, through his genetic memory, identifying with the Helix.

The Haitian had a vision of this winged serpent later in his life, and began wearing the symbol around his neck to remember the lessons of that folklore, and the father who told him the stories.

REPRESENTATIONS OF THE SYMBOL:

The Symbol in Jewelry/Clothing

Regardless of the source or interpretation of the symbol, one thing is clear: those with newly discovered or formed abilities feel a special connection to it. It may be explained through the genetic memory concept, but this connection is often represented through jewelry, including necklaces, rings, and earrings. Takezo Kensei had it emblazoned on his armor, sword, and banner. He even carried it as his banner. Jessica's tattoo (and later Peter's) is another form of physically displaying the symbol for all to see. The connection to it obviously runs deep.

Negative Representations

Despite the deep, seemingly profound connection the symbol has to those who have superhuman abilities, it has also been displayed in dark, more menacing fashions. Often the Helix has been scribbled or painted over the face of someone in a picture. Sylar was known to do this over the faces of people who had discovered their powers. He placed their pictures, defiled with the symbol over the face, on his map, before brutally killing each of them, taking their abilities.

A similar use of the symbol came at the hands of Adam, formerly known as Takezo Kensei. He sought revenge against the founding members of The Company for torturing and imprisoning him. He scratched the symbol in red over the faces of each member of The Company, and sent the picture to them as a warning that he would kill them. These uses of the symbol, as well as Sylar's, gave it a more threatening tone than it had ever had before.

CONCLUSION

No one knows the exact origin of the Helix symbol. Maybe its meaning is in the eye of the beholder, since it has meant something different to everyone who's encountered it.

To Ando, it was a simple combination of Japanese characters; to Hiro, the logo of his idol; to Niki, it's the manifestion of her murderous other self; for the Petrellis it was the symbol of their father's law-firm; to The Haitian, it represented the story of a winged serpent his father told him; Sylar saw it as new powers just waiting to be stolen; Adam saw it once as a godsend and then The Company that needed to be destroyed; and to the Bennets, it has meant constant change.

As the story unfolds so, perhaps, will the mystery surrounding the controversial symbol. But as different characters derive different meanings from it, and the Helix manifests itself in a myriad of ways, it will always stand, universally and simply, for *Heroes*. ∫

BACK TO THE FUTURE

A LOOK AT SEASON ONE, CHAPTER TWENTY: 'FIVE YEARS GONE'

SYNOPSIS

Hiro accidentally teleports himself and Ando into a future in which an explosion has destroyed New York. In Isaac's loft, they meet Future Hiro, who has created a huge string timeline to help figure out how to prevent the explosion. When Future Hiro learns that Peter saved the cheerleader, he realizes that Sylar can now be killed and says that Hiro must do the job. Homeland Security agents break in, led by Matt Parkman and The Haitian, and capture Hiro, mistaking him for Future Hiro.

Ando and Future Hiro get away and start planning a rescue. After trying and failing to enlist Peter's help, they meet with Mr. Bennet, who is running an underground network to hide undocumented Heroes. Mr. Bennet also refuses to help, until Ando reveals that they know Claire is still alive. Future Hiro and Ando are planning the rescue of Hiro, when Matt and his SWAT team break into the Primatech facility to capture them, and Matt realizes there are two Hiros. Peter appears, freezes time, and teleports Future Hiro and Ando away. Matt then betrays his secret alliance with Mr. Bennet. He takes Claire's location from Mr. Bennet's mind, shoots him, and goes to capture Claire.

Both Matt and Mohinder are reporting directly to President Nathan Petrelli, whose priorities are to stop whatever Future Hiro is planning, and to eliminate the

Hero gene from the human population. When Mohinder tells him that the genetic mutation can't be cured or reversed, Nathan orders him to plan for a genocide.

After talking with Hiro, Mohinder explains Future Hiro's plan to the President, who orders Mohinder to execute Hiro. The President then goes to see Claire, whom Matt has just brought in. She realizes too late that he is not her father, Nathan, but Sylar. He murders her and takes her power.

Peter reveals to his girlfriend, Niki, that he, not Sylar, was the exploding man. Peter, Future Hiro, and Ando head for New York to rescue Hiro and send him back so he can rewrite the past.

As "Nathan" leads a fifth anniversary memorial for those who died in New York, the rescuers attack the facility where Hiro is detained. Mohinder kills The Haitian instead of Hiro, and helps him escape. With The Haitian dead, Matt and his SWAT forces are overwhelmed by the combined powers of Future Hiro and Peter, and Matt desperately calls the President for back-up. Sylar abandons his disguise and flies away, in full view of millions, to join the fight. He reveals his true identity to Peter, and the two begin a titanic battle of energy powers. Just in time, Hiro teleports himself and Ando back to the present.

EPISODE STATS:

DETAILS: Chapter 20: *Five Years Gone*
VOLUME: One
ORIGINAL US AIRDATE: April 30, 2007
WRITER: Joe Pokaski
DIRECTOR: Paul Edwards

MAKING THE EPISODE

The *Heroes* creative team always knew *Five Years Gone* was going to be a big episode. From the earliest days of discussing the concept, the idea of a jump into the future excited the *Heroes* writing and production teams. Staff writer Joe Pokaski eventually ended up taking on the episode, and he vividly recalls its beginnings. "We started kicking around ideas for *Five Years Gone* as early as July 2006, during the San Diego Comic-Con. I remember being with Bryan Fuller, Michael Green, and Aron Coleite in a hotel room between panels, and because we are who we are, we couldn't stop talking about this episode and all the possibilities and permutations of our characters in the future."

The explosion that will destroy New York has been a threat since chapter two, though only Hiro believes in it at first. The writers knew as soon as they showed Future Hiro telling Peter to "Save the cheerleader, save the world," in chapter five, that they would eventually have to tell the story of what would happen if Peter failed.

Fifteen episodes later, *Five Years Gone* reveals that story. From the moment Future Hiro walks into the loft and pins his deadly glare on Hiro and Ando, we are in a different world. And it's a world where everything has gone wrong. Not only has New York been destroyed, but nearly all the good guys have lost their way: Hiro is a terrorist; Matt is a corrupt cop who beats and murders prisoners; Mohinder is helping the President find a way to wipe out those with special powers; and Peter, the sweet-natured guy who once wanted to save the world, is sitting this one out.

In the *Heroes* script-development process, the entire writing staff works on each episode, breaking all aspects of the story and writing an "assembly draft"

FACTS & TRIVIA

• The original episode title was *String Theory* (a title later used for the related graphic novel, chapter 30, which Pokaski also wrote). The writers changed it because they wanted a title that clearly showed the episode was set in a different time, similar to the title of the flashback episode *Six Months Ago*.

• The episode's director, Paul Edwards, also directed *Seven Minutes to Midnight* and *Kindred*. Writer Joe Pokaski also wrote *Fallout* and *Cautionary Tales*.

• The Oval Office set was previously used for the movie *Dave* and is exactly the same scale as the real Oval Office.

• The Explosion Memorial was inspired by the Vietnam Veterans' Memorial in Washington DC. It had over 1,000 names on it, including the names of virtually the entire *Heroes* crew repeated several times. The set was built in the parking lot outside the *Heroes* production offices.

• This episode was the first time that Sendhil Ramamurthy shot a scene with Greg Grunberg, who would become his roommate in season two. It was also the first time Masi Oka shot scenes with Jack Coleman and with Ramamurthy.

• Ramamurthy took three weeks to grow his beard for this episode. Alert fans may notice that his beard stubble is somewhat heavier in the preceding episodes.

• Adrian Pasdar worked with Zachary Quinto to create his performance as Sylar impersonating Nathan. Quinto even recorded all of "Nathan's" lines for Pasdar to study.

• Unusually, *Five Years Gone* ran so close to the required episode length that only one short scene had to be cut, which shows Future Hiro and Ando discussing H.R.G. This appears on the season one DVD set's Deleted Scenes section.

STRING THEORY

Future Hiro's string map is a central piece of the *Five Years Gone* story. It not only linked all the characters at critical moments, it created one of the season's most memorable visuals. Joe Pokaski recalls how it came to be...

"We were trying to find the coolest way for Future Hiro to really know why saving the cheerleader would save the world. Bryan Fuller was the first person to talk about the strings – I remember him explaining them like a spider-web in Isaac's loft. Tim Kring has always thought of Isaac's loft as one of several 'spiritual epicenters' of our universe – and putting the string in the loft felt right.

"From there I ran with it, and got my nerd on – really figuring out how you could chart time and lives with string. There were many graphs and tables involved.

It was a fun trip to the edge of insanity...

"The props department – specifically Reba Rosenthal – were so helpful in making that craziness a reality.

I kept waiting for them to call me out on how ridiculous the notion was – but instead they executed it perfectly."

In the future version of Isaac's loft, the center of the set was marked off by a circle of easels. All of the string map outside the circle was the responsibility of the set decoration crew, while the map within the circle was created by the props department, because the actors would be interacting with it. Reba Rosenthal explains her approach to a job which took several weeks...

"With the current TV viewers owning HD televisions and DVRs, we are challenged to ensure that everything that makes it to set is of the highest quality. For that reason, a lot of thought and care was put into the string map.

> ## "Future Hiro's string map created one of the season's most memorable visuals"

"We wanted each of the Heroes' strings to be three-dimensional timelines showing the evolution of the character. Items each character had used throughout the season were strung towards the center of the timeline where the explosion in New York was depicted. For the future, with help from the writers, we created items that we thought might happen to our characters over the course of five years after the explosion.

"We tried to use a different theme and color for each [character's] strings. Sylar's [black string] progression was shown through photos of people he had killed... Peter's [white] story was told through the images Isaac painted of him. Hiro's [red] string is told with items that he physically used during the show – like an origami crane from the diner scene with Charlie."

Rosenthal adds that the map originally included intersecting strings for all of the main characters. This proved too intricate to be practical in production, so five of the strings were removed, leaving only Sylar, Claire, H.R.G., Peter, Nathan, and Hiro. The outer areas of the map were also filled with "real" items like newspaper stories representing events in that future world.

To facilitate moving cameras and actors in and out of the central map, the easels were specially made so that the front of the frame could be removed. The outer web strings were always attached to the easel backs, while the inner strings were attached to the fronts. This way, sections of the inner web could be easily moved away just by unscrewing the front easel sections with the strings attached. Only a couple of shots could not be accomplished this way, and for these, the strings were inserted digitally afterwards.

together before handing it over to one writer for the final draft. For *Five Years Gone*, in addition to breaking a complex story, the writers had the extra challenge of coming up with each character's future.

"We made sure we knew who the characters were and what they had been through in these five years, even before we locked the story down," says Pokaski. "Tim [Kring], who, needless to say, completely understands these characters, was huge in helping develop these 'extrapolations of character.'"

The "extrapolations" led to many character reversals, such as Mr. Bennet working to hide people with powers, Peter and Niki as lovers, and Ando dead. Surprisingly, the biggest reversal of all, that Sylar has become "President Nathan Petrelli," was not part of the original concept. Pokaski recalls that he and fellow writer Aron Coleite were brainstorming

ideas for Nathan and Sylar, whose future stories seemed to them rather unsatisfying, when both hit on the notion of having Nathan *be* Sylar. This led to one of Pokaski's favorite aspects of the whole episode.

"I loved how the Nathan-is-Sylar reveal played over the hour," he says. "While we were shooting, we got to play with different levels of Sylar peeking through. The goal was that nearly nobody should see it coming on the first viewing, then everyone could see it clearly on the second viewing. And that's exactly what happened with a lot of the fans."

The writing of the script fell to Pokaski through what he calls, "Half dumb luck, half wishing really hard." In fact, it was his turn to write. As with the other out-of-sequence

MY HIROS

Hiro and Future Hiro appear together in only two scenes in *Five Years Gone*. Joe Pokaski and his fellow writers structured the story to keep the two apart, precisely so that production wouldn't be swamped by the technicalities of shooting a dual role. In most of the shots where both Hiros appear, either a split-screen effect was used, or the second Hiro was a body double with his back to the camera. These two techniques are so familiar that any viewer can spot them immediately as special effects.

To sell the reality of two Hiros in the same place, an early scene shows us the two Hiros *passing* each other across the frame. This shot, when Future Hiro walks

past Hiro and Ando to the window, then crosses back past Hiro again, was accomplished with motion control.

The motion control camera is a computerized camera and dolly which can duplicate precisely any camera angle and movement, so the exact shot can be repeated for as many takes as needed. Future Hiro's part was shot first, because he was moving and the camera had to follow him. Once an acceptable take of his motion had been done, Masi Oka changed costume to Hiro, and the entire scene was reshot, with Oka required, in each take, to hit his marks perfectly and pace his dialog to match the previous version of the shot. Director of photography Nate Goodman reported in an online interview that this one shot took *six hours* to accomplish.

episodes, he knew the events in this story had to have emotional resonance with the current character arcs in the main story.

"For me, the characters and their relationships are always the most important part of a script," he says. "In this particular script they were even more important – they needed to be as emotional and real as possible, because the context was so very *out there*.

"The Future Hiro and Ando relationship was really something I wanted to get right. We had the chance to tell the tale of a normally carefree 'boy' who lost his best friend, and how it hardened him around the edges and forced him to become a man. How saving his best friend was the whole seed that drove him to obsess about stopping the bomb. Then, when the friend comes back, he softens up a little. He remembers who he used to be. If I'm fortunate enough to do this job for

100 years, I may not get to tell a story quite like that again."

Filming *Five Years Gone* was a major production effort for all concerned (see boxouts). Fortunately, both the studio and the network were as excited by the episode's concept as the *Heroes* production team, and gave enthusiastic support for it. For a number of reasons, not least the logistics of having to schedule Masi Oka for shooting two versions of Hiro, the episode took much longer than usual to produce. Production on the next episode, *The Hard Part*, was already complete, and pre-production for chapter 22 was underway before the last scenes from *Five Years Gone* were finished.

Pokaski says, looking back at that enormous effort: "I'm proudest of the fact that we got to tell this story. That we just went for it. I'm a huge fanboy and live for television that pushes the limits: *E.R.*'s *Loves Labor Lost*, *Buffy the Vampire Slayer*'s *Hush*, that *M.A.S.H.* episode with the chicken at the back of the bus… These episodes had a 'because we can' attitude in swinging for the fences. I can definitely say with confidence that we swung for the fences on this one."

PETER THE GREAT

In Heroes, it would seem that Peter Petrelli has got it all – good looks, very interesting friends, and formidable powers. But then again, he has a corrupt family, equally powerful enemies, and a generally disastrous love-life. We caught up with actor Milo Ventimiglia to discuss his thoughts on the first two seasons of Heroes…

Versatile" is a word that can be applied to Peter Petrelli. As we've seen over two seasons of *Heroes*, the former hospice nurse can – depending on the situation and who he's been hanging around – fly, teleport, read minds, and generally adopt any superpowers he encounters. Milo Ventimiglia, who plays Peter, displays similar adaptability.

The native of Anaheim, California has not only played a wide variety of roles in a screen career that dates back to 1995 – when he appeared as a party guest on the Will Smith series *The Fresh Prince of Bel-Air* – but Ventimiglia has also started his own production company as a producer and director. As an actor, Ventimiglia has had regular gigs on *Opposite Sex* and a breakout role as the heroine's boyfriend on *The Gilmore Girls*. He's also played the title character's son in the feature film *Rocky Balboa* and a doctor involved with a ring of serial killers in the upcoming thriller *Pathology*. He's played a young version of Ken Olin's character on the series *Easy Street*, co-created by Bobby Moresco and Paul Haggis, whose film *Crash* went on to win the Best Picture Oscar.

But TV viewers worldwide now know Ventimiglia as Peter Petrelli, the noble nurse who has the power to, well, have any power. The character has been on an incredible journey in the two seasons so far – coming to terms with his powers, saving the world a couple of times, losing girlfriends in rather nasty ways – and those are just some of the goings-on. We found out more from the actor himself...

This spread, clockwise from left: Peter with love rival Isaac; Nathan visits Peter in prison; Peter and his season one fringe; Peter uses his powers in season two

Did you always want to be an actor?

MILO VENTIMIGLIA: When I was a little kid, I'd done plays. I was really into performing – people just kept telling me I was pretty good at it. So when I got to college at UCLA [University of California, Los Angeles], I did a theatre major and out of that I got a scholarship to a conservatory in San Francisco and then went into this business and soon realized that I could actually make a living out of doing it. As I've gotten older, my work has diversified and I've followed different interests within the [film/TV] industry.

How did you become involved in *Heroes*?

I was already on a TV show called *The Bedford Diaries* for Warner Brothers. I was in Philadelphia, working on a film for Sony [*Rocky Balboa*], and I got a phone call from Dave Semel,

"WHEN THE HEROES SCRIPTS COME IN, THEY'RE ALWAYS WAY BETTER THAN I EXPECTED."

the director of [the pilot for] *Heroes*. He and I worked together two years previous on a show called *American Dreams*. He said they were having a hard time finding an actor to play this part. They knew that I was already committed to something else, but asked if I would read the material and put myself on tape. I said, yeah, no problem. I put myself on tape [when] I was in New York, and I guess everybody back in L.A. responded to it and decided to bring me in, and that's when the network got excited about me. They really didn't care that I was on another show. They took their chances and it worked out to their benefit – *Heroes* got picked up and the other show did not. I wasn't necessarily looking for something [as a TV regular], but the opportunity presented itself and it was a chance to work on great material.

What appealed to you about Peter as a character?
There was a lot. He wasn't like a lot of the characters that I've played on television in the past couple years. He has a lot more depth and he's a little more caring of people around him. He has a lot of heart, but he isn't a pushover. He has drive, he has dreams – there was just a lot. Just the fact that he got to fly –

LOOKING THE PART

Whether he's saving cheerleaders or having a cheeky kiss, Peter always picks the right style. Let's take a look at some of his quintessential looks...

MEDICAL MARVEL
Not so long ago Peter was just a shy nurse, day-dreaming about leaping off buildings – but it's hard to imagine him saving the world in his nurse's uniform...

DRESSED TO IMPRESS
Unlike his brother, Nathan, it's rare that we get to see Peter making an effort. In *One Giant Leap* he goes all out for one of Nathan's campaign events in a suit and tie that land him in a lip-lock with Simone.

TALL COAT-TAILS
In the opening sequence of the pilot episode, we are treated to a beautiful shot of Peter diving off a New York tenement building. This fantastic feast for the eyes would not be complete without *that* coat, which flies out behind him like a superhero's cloak. Move over Superman – there's a new Hero in town!

SCARRED FOR LIFE
In the shocker that was *Five Years Gone*, Peter appears with a harsh new look. Complete with full facial battle-scar, tight white vest and slicked-back hair – this hardcore version of the soft-centered Peter we've come to know and love looks like he's been through some tough times.

SHORT AND SHARP
New season, new look. It's all short back and sides and dark threads for Peter when Elle gives him a trim and he chucks those preppy shirts and khaki trousers in the trash. We bid farewell to the youthful floppy mop and embraced an older, wiser-looking Mr. Petrelli. After all, you can't worry about hair getting in your eyes when there's a world to save.

THE SKIN HE'S IN
It would be rude not to give Peter's pecs a mention here. (Also recommended for optimum pectoral viewing are season one's *Collision* and season two's *Lizards*...)

Left: Peter, captured and topless, at the start of season two; Peter saves the cheerleader in season one

MILO MOMENTS

Although his career as an actor is flourishing, Milo Ventimiglia is branching out into producing and directing with his production company, Divide Pictures, serving as chief executive officer with partners Russ Cundiff and Michael Ryan-Fletchall. Divide has so far produced several shorts, including a series of commercials for clothing company American Eagle Outfitters; a feature film is in the pipeline.

"I directed 65 minutes of content for American Eagle," Ventimiglia explains. "It's 12 five-minute shorts. Basically, American Eagle Outfitters is acting as a studio and distribution company. They hired my production company to come up with some content, something that they're going to release on their website. It's also going to go on MTV first. They wanted to get into the realm of television and film production, reminiscent of when you see a company like BMW doing [the series of *Driver* shorts with Clive Owen], putting out something for consumers. It was something that Adam Green wrote, it's a comedy, shot very much like a television show in HD [high-definition video]; we use the Panasonic NC-HD."

The ensemble nature of *Heroes* has been a boon to Ventimiglia's behind-the-camera work, he notes. "I have actually nothing but good feelings about it. Being on a show where you're one of the singular lead roles is a lot of work. It's tiring – the physical hours you're on set, learning your lines and taking care of yourself, it's just a lot of responsibility. I was completely thrilled about going into *Heroes* – going into an ensemble cast. [With this many] people sharing the responsibility, we're going to have plenty of time to work, but at the same time, we have plenty of time off to take care of ourselves and catch up on other endeavors."

I thought, "Well, that's kind of cool." I just saw this dynamic relationship between Nathan and Peter, and it was Peter aiding his brother Nathan and discovering that he could fly. It wasn't until a couple of months later, after the show had been picked up and we were all in New York at the upfronts, and Tim [Kring] walked up to me and he had a big smile on his face and said, "I think we've figured out Peter." And then he dove into his explanation of what Peter's ability was. In the pilot episode, he doesn't fly so much as plummet! He's showing his brother Nathan that [Nathan] has the power to do that, to fly. My character is an empath. He feels people's true emotions and their true potential.

Did you do any research into either the paranormal or nursing aspects of Peter's character before you started filming?

There is a responsibility to work on a character

on your own outside of what's written. The medic stuff I started to research online and actually went to a couple of hospitals just to watch, just to look – not so much to be engaged with the nurses and trying to figure out exactly how to tie a tourniquet, put in an I.V., but just understanding what a hospice nurse goes through. My grandfather passed away – he was under hospice care years ago – and I remember trying to recall how [my grandfather's hospice nurse] came in. They weren't so sterile and routine, I think, as hospitals can be. They actually have a lot of warmth and generosity about them in the way they approach their patients, which was nice to see. I didn't get into the paranormal aspect of it, because it wasn't so defined and Peter was unaware of his powers [at the beginning]. Even though he felt like he could fly, he had no idea that he was empathetically feeling people.

Did you fantasize about being a superhero when you were a kid?

Yeah, of course. When you're a kid, everybody runs around with a red cape – we all wanted to be Superman or Batman, I think, in the comic book fashion of a superhero. I grew up on comics and I was more into Batman and The Punisher, guys that actually didn't have out-of-this-world abilities, they were just kind of crazy and had a [righteous] kind of response. But of course – Superman or Spider-Man – any of those characters were exciting, too. But as you get older, you get into the logistics of it a little more, like, would I rather be able to fly, or would I rather be invisible, and how fast can I fly, and how much can I control my invisibility? I think it's a natural human interest to look into things like that. I think if I could have a superhero power, I would actually want the power of persuasion. It sounds kind of odd, but think about it. You

BROTHERS GRIM?

What is it like playing the brother of Adrian Pasdar's Nathan?
MILO VENTIMIGLIA: Sometimes you'll be working on a highly emotional scene and you'll get lost in the fact that you're actually having fun with your friend. You have an opportunity to give as much to them as they give back to you. It's not lost on Adrian and I. When we finish a scene, we just kind of look at each other and start laughing. We have this great opportunity to have a good time and give it as much as we can. I know that Adrian gives so much to me, and I'll be damned if I'm not going to give that back to him.

"I WASN'T NECESSARILY LOOKING FOR SOMETHING AS A TV REGULAR, BUT THE OPPORTUNITY PRESENTED ITSELF AND HEROES WAS A CHANCE TO WORK ON GREAT MATERIAL."

This pic: Peter chooses the wrong side – allying himself with Adam Monroe – in season two

could end wars, you could do a lot.

You could talk people out of committing violent acts...
Absolutely. Placing a [person with powers] like that in strategic places might benefit the world.

What are your favorite Peter Petrelli scenes?
How can you rate a favorite? They're all pretty good and they all explore different things. It's hard to pick. I think there were definitely moments I had with all the actors. To be a character that got to work with almost everybody – I worked with Hayden, I worked with Jack, I worked with Sendhil, I worked with Masi, I worked with Zach, Adrian, Greg, Ali – I worked with everybody. That was the fun for me, ➡

was to just jump around.

Are you excited to read the new scripts as they come in?

Yeah. When Adrian [Pasdar] and I see that we're getting to fly, the first thing we say is, "Ouch." The second is, "Cool!" We get one or two writers who'll sneak down to the set and go, "Dude, you've got some cool stuff coming up, but you're going to be working your ass off." When you first read the script, there's this basic human emotion and these wonderfully-written characters interacting. Of course, it's definitely cool to do the non-reality stuff that we do. When they're writing it, when they're putting it on the page – the way they describe it – your mouth is open in awe. Like when they first describe Adrian flying: "He just rockets right into the sky, before you can say, 'Best show on television.'"

Is there anything you'd like to see Peter do in the new season?

I approach it like everyday life. There are hopes and ideals of where you can be and what you may be doing, but they're not always going to happen. The scripts could come out and you really have no expectations. You have a couple of conversations with Tim Kring and Jeph [Loeb] and the writers, but for me personally, I like to try to focus on the page and the work at hand and have a broader, very vague idea of what's coming up and then when the scripts come in, they're always

"WHEN YOU'RE A KID, EVERYBODY RUNS AROUND WITH A RED CAPE – WE ALL WANTED TO BE SUPERMAN OR BATMAN."

better than I ever expected them to be.

Have you personally experienced much of the public reaction to *Heroes*?

I can honestly walk down the street, go in a grocery store, eat in a restaurant – it's all pretty much the same. I get a couple more people saying, "Hey, I love your show," or "Hey, you're from that show." Nothing much different. I hear from friends all the time – you're walking down the street and pass a couple arm in arm who are talking about Niki this, Nathan that, Hiro this, Ando that. It seems just the overall response to the show, hearing that, is coming from so many different walks of life. It's nice to know that, hopefully, we're doing our jobs well enough that people talk about them at the workplace or at home or with friends.

Why do you think *Heroes* appeals to people so much?

I think it's just the subject matter and it's kind of the state of the world. People are just interested to see good characters with unusual circumstances. The young and

THE HEART OF A HERO

There's no denying it – Peter Petrelli has been lucky with the ladies. We look at who's locked lips with _Heroes'_ hottest power-wielding Romeo...

SIMONE DEVEAUX

Art dealer Simone was the first girl to steal Peter's heart on the show. While nursing her sick father, Charles, Peter falls for the feisty brunette who's dating artist and fellow Hero, Isaac Mendez. In season one's _One Giant Leap,_ he confesses his love for her and they end up kissing beneath the infamous red umbrella, as Isaac's painting predicted. They spend the night together and with Simone's relationship with Isaac falling apart, she turns to Peter for support. Sadly, any chance at a future with Simone is shattered when Isaac accidentally shoots her in _Unexpected_ and she dies in Peter's arms.

NIKI SANDERS

In _Five Years Gone_ we are shown a bleak future where vigilante Peter is forced to hide away in Vegas. Future Peter's one solace is Niki, his girlfriend. After losing Micah and D.L. in the explosion, Niki is working as a stripper under her Jessica alter ego. Her relationship with Peter is cold and uncertain, both of them still suffering from the events that occurred five years before. We see a tender moment between them and a passionate kiss, but when Peter reveals he was the one who caused the explosion and that he has to help Hiro change the past she gives him an ultimatum, and he decides saving the world is more important than saving their relationship.

ELLE BISHOP

In season two, electric Elle finds herself in the lucky position of guarding Peter as The Company develop a "cure" for his powers. She finds him irresistible and sparks fly (for her at least!). But when Peter and Adam decide to escape in _Four Months Ago,_ Peter uses the bad girl's weakness for him against her – lulling her into a false sense of security. He lies, telling her he's starting to like her and her "shock" tactics before giving her a high-voltage kiss. Seconds later he's spitting out his medication and walking through walls to freedom. To her, he'll always be the one that got away.

CAITLIN

There's nothing like the love of a hot-headed Irish lass to help a Hero through the dark times. At the start of season two, Peter finds himself in Ireland without his memory (or his shirt), so the lips of friendly barmaid Caitlin are a welcome relief from the drama of this Hero's life. Peter learns to trust her and her brother Ryan, and ends up moving in to her apartment and painting a prophetic picture that shows the two of them in Montreal. They head off to avenge Ryan's death but this isn't the romantic holiday Caitlin was probably hoping for as an accidental teleport to New York results in her being stranded in a virus-ridden future. Will he ever see his Irish beauty again...?

Top: Peter with new friend Hiro; Below: Peter with niece Claire; Far left: An amnesiac Peter tries to put his life back together in season two; This pic: Peter in Montreal – where his life is aobut to change forever...
Next page, top: Peter and tragic girlfriend Caitlin; Below: Hiro attacks Peter for siding with Adam

the old – it's kind of funny. My friend's grandmother, who is 88, watches the show. Her favorite character is Claire. I don't think there's one storyline that plays to a younger audience and another that plays to an older audience. I think overall you have to look at it, and collectively, you see that there's something for everybody. And ultimately, every storyline is appealing to an 88-year-old woman, as well as a teenager or somebody in their 20s, 30s, or 40s. I think there's not one storyline or one character that plays more to an audience than the next. So any storyline can be enjoyed by everybody.

What do you think of science fiction/fantasy as a genre?

I think it's cool. My science fiction knowledge – I wouldn't say it starts and stops with *Star Wars*, but I think there's such a wide open world. Science fiction really allows for the unexplainable, as opposed to the more rational way of proving science. In science fiction, anything can happen. It can be made up, it could be true, it could not be true. I think there's a lot of

MILO VENTIMIGLIA SELECTED CREDITS

TV

Heroes – Peter Petrelli (2006-present)
The Bedford Diaries – Richard Thorne III (2006)
Gilmore Girls – Jess Mariano (2004-2006)
American Dreams – Chris Pierce (2004-2005)
Law & Order: Special Victims Unit – Lee Healy (2003)
Boston Public – Jake (2003)
CSI: Crime Scene Investigation – Bobby Taylor (2000)
Opposite Sex – Jed Perry (2000)
Promised Land – Tony Brackett (1999)
One World – Eric (1998)
Rewind – Young Rob (1997)
Sabrina, the Teenage Witch – Letterman (1996)
The Fresh Prince of Bel-Air – Party Guest (1995)

MOVIES

Pathology – Ted Gray (2008)
Rocky Balboa – Robert Jr. (2006)
Stay Alive – Loomis Crowley
Intelligence – Colin Mathers (2006)
Dirty Deeds – Zach Harper (2005)
Cursed – Bo (2005)
Winter Break – Matt Raymand (2003)
Nice Guys Finish Last – Josh (2001)
Speedway Junkie – Travis (1999)
She's All That – Soccer Player (1999)
Must Be the Music – Jason (1996)

"HOPEFULLY, WE'RE DOING OUR JOBS WELL ENOUGH THAT PEOPLE TALK ABOUT *HEROES* AT THE WORKPLACE OR AT HOME OR WITH FRIENDS."

possibility in it and I'm happy to be on a show that falls not only under science fiction but falls in the real world, too. There is, of course, the element of superhero/superpowers, but what it is, is happening to everyday people. These people are normal, just like you or I. There's that fear and that exhilaration of understanding about these powers – you can accomplish such great things or you can destroy great things. So I think it's kind of cool to mix the two worlds. I think it widens the door of who we get to reach. The approach [as an actor] is pretty much the same. Whether it's science fiction or a more reality-based project, there's human emotion, unless you're playing an android or an alien. But other than that, I look at it as the same. I play the character the best I can and make sure it's a good representation of the person that I'm playing.

What's been the best thing about *Heroes* for you so far?

The execution of the show and the collective, talented nature of everybody involved in the crew – everybody is really going in such a linear motion that it would be hard for it not to do well. Being on set, you see so many talented people working really hard and working really well together.

THE POWERS THAT BE

A look at PETER PETRELLI'S abilities

First manifestation:

Peter first becomes aware of his ability in his dreams, which tell him he can fly (possibly caused by the amount of time he spends with his brother, the "Flying Man"). Peter uses an ability deliberately for the first time when he jumps off the roof to prove to Nathan that he can fly. He really starts to understand the nature of his gift when he realizes he's also absorbed Isaac's power of precognition.

The powers:

Peter's DNA re-sequences itself to mimic the abilities of other Heroes around him. Mohinder Suresh describes Peter as a kind of power sponge. Peter doesn't just mimic others' abilities while he's near them (like a chameleon blending in with its current environment), he retains each ability permanently (like an artist's sponge soaking up different paint colors). And apparently, he doesn't have to be in close proximity for his DNA to work its magic. He was many yards away from D.L., Niki, Micah, and Molly during the fight at Kirby Plaza, yet he seems to have absorbed all of their abilities – though so far he has only used D.L.'s phasing, and maybe Niki's super-strength when he was fighting Sylar in the plaza.

Maximum potential:

Theoretically, Peter's potential to absorb and master new powers is unlimited. So far, he's absorbed 20 distinct abilities, if not more. He currently uses fewer than half of these, and probably isn't even aware of the others (for a full list of Peter's powers, see the overview in Powers to the People, page 47). Mental control is essential in the use and development of most powers, so Peter can't consciously draw on abilities he doesn't know he has. His unconscious mind does seem able to tap into all of them, as in *Four Months Later*, when his 'fight or flight' reflex calls on powers he can't even remember. These latent powers don't seem to surface spontaneously in a non-emergency. Otherwise, Micah's ability to talk to machines would have helped Peter open the Company vault in Odessa with a lot less time and effort (just as well he didn't know how to use it, or

Adam would have gotten to the virus much more quickly!). Peter seems to master the abilities he does know about more and more easily, helped by Claude's training and also from absorbing Sylar's original power of understanding complex systems. As he grows in experience and understanding of his gift, Peter will probably learn to recognize a new power the moment he absorbs it, and begin to take control of each new power immediately. He could become a truly powerful Hero.

Maximum power:

Peter's most impressive use of his powers so far is in the post-explosion future of *Five Years Gone*. Future Peter, scarred, battle-hardened, and experienced in the assimilation of many abilities, uses a barrage of different powers with superhero speed, skill, and versatility, to fight off Matt Parkman's SWAT team, lead the assault on the New York facility, and finally go head-to-head with the villainous, power-stealing Sylar.

How the Power Changes His Life:

Peter has grown up in the shadow of his father and big brother – the "alpha dogs" of the family – underrated by those who should love and value him the most, especially his mother.

All his life, he has wanted to make the world a better place – but not in the way of his parents and his brother, the way of politics and power, which is as much about ego as about public service. Peter chose to be a nurse because he wanted to help people, even if it was just in his own small way. The discovery of his powers, and especially the mission Future Hiro gives him, to "save the cheerleader, save the world", gives Peter the hope that he may be able to help in a big way. As much as he needs to understand his growing powers, he needs even more to feel that he's part of some important destiny, something much bigger than himself.

The burden that goes with this new responsibility is Peter's fear of his own weaknesses. He is afraid to fail at the mission, afraid that he's not good enough to become a true Hero and save the world. And worst of all, he's afraid that his sometimes terrifying powers might become the means to destroy the world.

Biggest Danger:

Mohinder warns Nathan that Peter's gift could become dangerous if he absorbs an unstable ability or absorbs too many powers at once. The first time he absorbs multiple powers in a short time (Claire's, Matt's, and all of Sylar's) it makes him sick, and he's comatose for weeks. The second time doesn't kill him, but it almost kills everyone else in New York. Only a short time after he has absorbed Ted Sprague's highly unstable radioactive power, Peter is exposed to the new powers of Molly, Micah, Niki, and D.L., and his marginal control of Ted's power is overwhelmed.

Only Nathan flying him up into the atmosphere saves him from nuking the city. Given exposure to another forceful and destructive power (like Maya's, perhaps), or even to another large number of Heroes at once, Peter could lose control again and cause some unimaginable disaster to himself or those around him.

Great power like Peter's, of course, carries another great risk. Sylar, Elle, and Maury Parkman have already given us a taste of the nastiness that ensues when powerful Heroes use their abilities to hurt and control people. Peter will have to be an extraordinary soul to escape the temptation of his enormous power, and the seduction of using it to make others do what he thinks is for the greater good. In the short term, Peter's great capacity for love may make him even more dangerous to those who have attacked the person he loves most in the world. Who knows what the most powerful Hero on Earth might do to punish the assassins of his brother Nathan?

UNANSWERED QUESTIONS

Regarding the regenerative power: Did Peter absorb any new or different aspects of it from Adam? Can he, like Adam, potentially be immortal? Does his blood have the same curative powers as that of Claire and Adam? Could he be immune to the Shanti virus, in all its deadly variations?

Regarding the precognitive power: Isaac was an artist, so it was easy and natural for his power to manifest itself through his art. But we don't know if that's the only way it can work. Could Peter learn to draw on the precognition directly through his mind, without even needing a pencil or brush?

Regarding The Haitian's powers: The Haitian is the only Hero who can stop Peter from absorbing his abilities, simply by using them before Peter is close enough to mimic them. Did he ever give Peter a chance to absorb his abilities? Think how useful that power of suppression would be, the next time Peter comes face-to-face with Sylar!

Looking Badass:

When Mr. Bennet and The Haitian come to capture Peter and Claude, Peter freezes time and their taser electrodes, throws the paralyzed Claude off the roof, then dives after him, catches him and flies up, up and away, leaving the two very capable Hero-hunters standing. It's a quick-thinking, resourceful, perfectly coordinated use of multiple powers. Where's the kid who couldn't get out of his own way two days before?

Best Use of Powers:

Peter uses his telekinetic ability to catch the vial of deadly Strain 138 just before it shatters on the floor. Then he uses his radioactive fire to burn the vial and the virus into harmless dust. Humanity's saved again! For now…

Worst Use of Powers:

Is it the time he nearly blew up New York, or the time he helped Adam to get into the vault…? Guess again. Even when he's helping Adam, Peter believes he's doing the right thing to save the world, so he does his heroic best. His worst moment comes a few days earlier, in Dublin, when he telekinetically strangles Ricky's treacherous partner, Will. He only stops short of murdering the now-helpless thug when Caitlin intervenes. Peter tells her afterwards that in that moment, he wanted to murder Will; and he's terrified that his true identity might be that of a killer.

Biggest Act of Heroism:

Peter goes to Claire's rescue at Homecoming, getting between her and Sylar while she runs to safety. He keeps trying to delay Sylar even after he's had a taste of Sylar's power, and long before he knows his own. Finally, when Sylar grabs him to kill him and put him out of the way, he grabs back, and throws both Sylar and himself over a five-storey drop. Crunch! And he didn't even know he would regenerate and survive the fall. No wonder he's Claire's Hero!

BEAUTIFUL DREAMER

Though Peter originally believes that Nathan's power of flight is the first ability he absorbed, there is almost certainly an earlier one…

What is it?
At first, it looks like clairvoyant dreaming, because it manifests only when Peter is asleep or unconscious. With the first manifestations, he tells Nathan he has dreams of flying. He also witnesses Nathan's car accident while he's sleeping, and takes the dying Charles Deveaux on a flight around the city. He believes both of these events are also dreams. But as the power gets stronger, it begins to push through into Peter's waking mind. In the holding cell at Odessa, he has a conversation with Nathan which appears real to him until Nathan morphs into Sylar, then vanishes, and Peter realizes he's alone. Finally, he makes a real journey through time and space, from present day Montreal to future New York, and witnesses his own arrival there with Caitlin. When he returns to the present, Adam claims he never left the room, until Peter shows him an Evacuation notice he picked up in the future. His new power seems to be astral projection, the ability to project his consciousness out of his body.

How does it work?
Peter's spirit often seems to know, subconsciously, where it needs to travel and what it needs to show him, to provide vital information. It takes him to his brother's accident, and to talk with his friend Charles, who affirms his calling; it shows him warnings that he will be the

Exploding Man, and shows him the Invisible Man, Claude, who will teach him to control his abilities.

Most people can't see him leave his body, nor see his astral self when it visits them elsewhere. The exception is Charles, who may have had some psychic ability of his own. Perhaps others with psychic abilities, like the Parkmans, could also see the astral Peter. Peter's astral conversations with non-psychics may happen only when they are unconscious: Sylar was asleep or sedated the night Peter was in the holding cell, and Nathan was probably asleep at the time too.

What is its potential?
Like Hiro's teleportation power, Peter's ability to project himself (and the accompanying ability to determine what's important enough for him to see it) will probably grow more powerful and more precise with practice. He could potentially learn to travel out of body to any time or place he chooses, interact with other people both conscious and unconscious, and maybe even learn to take others with him on his journeys.

Where did it come from?
Though Charles Deveaux seems a likely source – because of his ability to see and talk with astral Peter – Peter actually saw Nathan's accident before he ever met Charles. We know of only one other (possible) Hero as close to Peter as Nathan, whose power he could have absorbed even before Nathan's: his mother, Angela…

SUPER FLY GUY

OF ALL THE HEROES WE MET AT THE OUTSET OF THE SHOW, POLITICAL CANDIDATE NATHAN PETRELLI WAS ONE OF THE MOST RELUCTANT TO ACCEPT HIS POWERS. BUT EXPOSURE TO THE MACHIAVELLIAN SCHEMES OF HIS OWN MOTHER AND THE COMPANY, AS WELL AS THE GOODNESS OF PETER AND CLAIRE, GAVE HIM A REASON TO SOAR UP, UP AND AWAY. THE ACTOR WHO PLAYS HIM, ADRIAN PASDAR, TALKS ABOUT FACING HIS FEARS, WHY NATHAN FLIES THE WAY HE DOES, AND WHETHER WE'VE SEEN THE LAST OF PETER'S BIG BROTHER...

This pic: Nathan with Company boss Bob. Right: Nathan gets ready to fight Matt Parkman's father

At a harbor in California's Santa Monica Bay, Adrian Pasdar, who plays *Heroes*' flying politician Nathan Petrelli, is on his boat – which often serves as a rehearsal space for the scenes between the Petrelli brothers. "Milo [Ventimiglia, who plays Peter Petrelli] and I spend a lot of time together prior to getting on set," Pasdar explains. "A lot of times beforehand, we'll get together at four in the morning and meet on my boat and go out to sea and we'll just keep running [the scene] and find the unexpected dynamic between the two of us in a scene through the course of repetition. Unfortunately, with TV, you just don't get a chance to rehearse, so we've made it a point to make sure that we make time to repeat it as often as we can, to sort out the bad stuff and unearth the good stuff."

Pasdar has been giving audiences the good stuff for a number of years now, in many capacities. A native of Massachusetts who was raised in Pennsylvania, Pasdar got a sports scholarship to college, but was injured and subsequently took up acting. He got into feature films with his first role as Chipper in *Top Gun*. Several subsequent roles – as a farm boy taken in by a band of vampires in *Near Dark* and as an unusual lawyer in TV's *Profit* – soon earned Pasdar a cult following.

He's also been a series regular on the courtroom drama *Judging Amy* and the supernatural thriller *Mysterious Ways*, as well as serving as writer and director on the film *Cement*, before becoming involved with *Heroes*.

Despite his long track record in acting, however, Pasdar had to audition for the role of Nathan. "I'll never forget it. There were a few people ahead of me and I had another appointment, and I asked these two gentlemen [who were also auditioning] if I might go ahead of them, and they said, 'Sure,' and halfway through the reading, I realized I had the job. It was one of those moments when you just know. I walked out of there and the phone started ringing as soon as I got to my car. So I don't know whether I would have got the job or one of those gentlemen who let me go ahead of them would have got the job. I'm not going to question it."

The initial impression Nathan made on Pasdar was that he was like, "a salesman. Tim Kring, the creator [of *Heroes*], explained to me that he wanted one of the characters who's going through this meta-morphosis to be in the public eye and have to deal with it on a personal level and also on a public level. Clearly, he can't make it public and traipse around the world flying, so I think there's a certain fear of ridicule. As Tim explained it, we've got a morally fluid character

"WHAT REALLY DICTATED THE WAY THAT I WAS FLYING WAS THAT I DIDN'T WANT MY PAJAMA BOTTOMS TO FALL OFF!"

who services the people and ideologies that are closest to him and most important to him and his family. Initially, in the first season, I think he really did believe all the choices he needed to make were the right ones, even if it ultimately meant sacrificing the small for the greater good, and I think there's a kind of disillusionment that happened over season one.

"For season two, [Nathan has been] coming close to the point where he's going to end up doing only the things that he believes are 100 percent right — not just long-term right, but also short-term right. The writing and the way that they've made the progression of this character has not been an expected journey. I've constantly been pleasantly surprised by the choices that they've made, script-wise — it's never been the obvious choice."

Then there are character traits that have come about for reasons that are *really* not obvious, like Nathan's flying style. "That wasn't even talked about until we were about to film it," Pasdar reveals. "There are only so many ways you're going to fly. What really dictated the way that I was flying was that I didn't want my pajama bottoms to fall off! I had one hand down, and then that didn't work out so well, because I jumped up in the air — I had to have

THE MAN FROM ATLANTA

Heroes hasn't confined Adrian Pasdar to television — while working on the series, he also starred in and served as one of the producers and camera operators (!) on the independent thriller *Home Movie*. "[It's about] a family that moves out into the wilderness and has to restructure their relations with each other once they realize that the two kids may or may not be serial killers," Pasdar explains.

Additionally, Pasdar co-wrote with musician Marcus Hummon and co-directed with Randall Arney the stage musical *Atlanta*, which played for seven weeks at the Geffen Playhouse in Los Angeles; there are now hopes of a London production and eventually a move to Broadway.

Atlanta is set in the last days of the American Civil War. It follows a Union soldier who winds up in disguise with a Confederate Army unit, commanded by a colonel who has his slaves perform works of the Bard.

"I can't think of anything harder than trying to contribute to the landscape of American musical theatre," Pasdar says. "It's a substantive piece that has

a very interesting draw, for me, being that it's about romance and racism with a backdrop of the Civil War, but it's still as contemporary a piece as I think you can find, in terms of its themes. We did four or five shows for [children from] the Los Angeles Unified School District, which is one of the great privileges that we had. We had Q & As [after the performance], and they would ask the most insightful questions."

One of the cast-members is Pasdar's erstwhile *Heroes* colleague Leonard Roberts, who played the late D.L. Hawkins. "I talked to him about [*Atlanta*] early on and thought he'd be great for it," Pasdar relates, "but I wasn't in a position to dictate who was going to be cast, so he had to go through the entire [audition] process. At the end of that first day of auditions, we had a list of who were the best people who came in. I kept my mouth shut and everybody else submitted their lists and he was on the top. He earned that part. It wasn't through anything I did. I wanted him more than anything in the world — he was perfect for it."

Other *Heroes* folks have cheered on the musical, Pasdar adds. "Tim [Kring] and [fellow *Heroes* writer/executive producer] Jeph Loeb have been very supportive through the entire run of *Atlanta* — they're very vested in creativity. They really like to see how things can unfold in whatever medium it is."

Pasdar's family has offered input as well. "My six-year-old kid saw the play and asked me, 'Daddy, why, in the beginning, did you start off with that loud clap of thunder? That scared me a little bit.' And I said, 'Well, the idea there is that we would try to clear whatever thoughts you had in your mind walking into the theatre and bring you right into the moment. Whatever you're thinking about, you instantly forget when you hear thunder.' And he looked at me and said, 'What if you were thinking about the play?'" Pasdar laughs. "That's the beauty of a six-year-old mind. He doesn't have things that he wants to forget that adults would bring in. It shows how important it is to write with that sense of innocence."

both hands down, pressed to my sides, to make sure that my shorts didn't fall off," he laughs. "The first time we ever did the flying, I was running on the roof in that scene where Jack Coleman's HRG is chasing me with The Haitian. They've rousted me out of bed, so I was in my pajama bottoms. It was just an elastic band around the waist. The drawstring had been taken out, because it was flopping around while I was running. I had to hold my hands down while I jumped, otherwise the pants would come down every time. I just didn't want to be flying through the air naked."

In *Heroes'* second season, Pasdar had to grow a real beard and contend with radiation burn make-up for Nathan's flashbacks and hallucinations. "That was a lot of fun," Pasdar reports. "It's always fun to put on a mask. It was fun to grow the beard and have that physical change be a part of the evolvement of the character. And the burn make-up – I'd go to work at four [in the morning]; I'd sit through five hours of make-up. You really can't move at all and you can't talk, you can't read a book – there's not a lot you can do, except contemplate what's happening to you physically. There's a big portion of it where you have to keep your eyes closed, and then you open them again after awhile and you've made this leap in [your] appearance. When you take a head mold [so the make-up artists have a cast of the actor to model the burn appliances on] – Hayden [Panettiere, as Nathan's indestructible biological daughter Claire] and I have had to do this for the show – they're very careful

RELUCTANT HERO

Unlike Peter Petrelli, who felt like a Hero before he even realized he was one, his older brother Nathan's always taken a little longer to settle into his heroic stride. With one of the coolest, most sought-after powers going, he spent most of season one being so fly-shy it took his brother's dramatic roof-top plunge to get him off the ground. But what was he so afraid of, and why was he so reluctant to make the most of his built-in boosters and jet off around the globe? We take a look at Nathan's reluctant *Heroes* adventure.

In Denial
When Peter dives off a building to prove he can fly, Nathan super-powers his way to his brother's rescue. But when Peter comes round in hospital, his big bro denies any knowledge of the incident, refusing to accept his remarkable ability.

Vote Petrelli
Despite finally admitting to Peter that he can fly, Nathan's fear of the public's response to an airborne politician overtakes him, and in *One Giant Leap* he puts family loyalty to one side and outs Peter to the press as a suicidal depressive in order to explain his "fall". This creates a divide between the brothers that continues for the majority of season one.

Brotherly Love?
Just when you think Nathan is going to step up to the plate and be a hero by shooting Linderman in the head (unknowingly taking out a member of The Company), his desire to be President gets in the way. In *.07%*, Linderman persuades him that it is Peter's destiny to die in the explosion and that, with his help, Nathan's future can be in the White House.

Bad Dad
Rather than taking his responsibilities as a Hero and a father seriously, Nathan puts winning the election above being there for Claire and his brother. Seeing Isaac's picture of him standing in the Oval Office is too tempting to ignore, and when Claire and Peter say they're going to try and stop the explosion, he turns to Linderman for help.

On the Drink
Season two's defeated Nathan is a stark contrast to the confident politician from season one. The "loss" of his brother and the departure of his wife have taken their toll on the ex-congressman, who has become an alcoholic struggling to find the Hero within. It takes a forceful Matt Parkman and the arrest of his mother to make Nathan realize that he must do something to prevent future disasters.

Taking the Cape
It's not all bad news, however. Nathan may have let his family down and lost his morals along the way, but at the end of season one he was instrumental in helping Peter save the world – using his super-fast flying ability to whisk Peter into space, risking his own life. And in season two's *Powerless*, he fights to bring down The Company and puts everything on the line to tell the world about his power, finally admitting who he is and what he's capable of – only to then be shot. He's a reluctant Hero, but a true one, all the same.

not to cover the holes in your nose, but that's all you're breathing through. And I am a little bit claustrophobic, so that eight minutes and 35 seconds, completely immobile with this head mold on, was a very interesting time. My heart was beating like a rabbit, and you can't move and you can't hear anything. I scuba-dive, I'm certified as a rescue diver – all that stuff's fine when I'm in

In an interview in *The Official Heroes Magazine*, Cristine Rose, who plays Nathan's mother Angela, said that Pasdar and Greg Grunberg would make her laugh uncontrollably whenever they were together. It's true, says Pasdar. "She is such a peculiar, funny, talented woman. I've never met anyone like her, and she's so up our alley when it comes to the kind of humor that Greg and I share that she's

afternoon, we were still doing the same scene and we were all just on our last legs. I mean, we were just giggling at anything. There's been a lot of that good humor [from] all of us. And Cristine, fortunately for us, has been present for a lot of it and she's been a great release valve for Greg and myself."

Working with Ventimiglia is another aspect of *Heroes* that Pasdar loves. "We started off really close, and just with a kinship and respect for each other, and that's just evolved into, I think, a greater understanding of the other person's rhythms and a greater understanding, ultimately, I think, of what's possible between those two people on-screen. But it's been really rewarding for me to be with him off-screen. It's been a great, positive influence on my life. He's a completely admirable fellow and there's a good chunk of me that's been made better by my friendship with him."

"MILO'S A COMPLETELY ADMIRABLE FELLOW AND THERE'S A GOOD CHUNK OF ME THAT'S BEEN MADE BETTER BY MY FRIENDSHIP WITH HIM."

control of it and I can see. But when you're just sitting in a chair with that hot [alginate] that's drying on your face, it's a little bit intimidating. But I got through it and I think I grew a little bit. I mean, there's nothing more exhilarating than having a chance to face your fears, and I just felt like that experience allowed me to overcome an obstacle that I had never had a chance to face before."

always our first target. We always like to see if we can crack her up, because it's so rewarding – she's so honest with her laughing. She can't stop, literally. We've all had moments like that on this set. Some of the best I've ever had are with Greg and with Milo. We had a scene that we had to film in the vault, where [Peter] catches the vial. That was about 9.30 in the morning, and at about 5.30 that

Season two's arc, Pasdar feels, has been necessary for *Heroes* as a whole. "I think when season two is put together on DVD and looked back on as part of that collective story in, say, five years, when

> "I THINK NATHAN REALLY DID BELIEVE ALL THE CHOICES HE NEEDED TO MAKE WERE THE RIGHT ONES, EVEN IF IT ULTIMATELY MEANT SACRIFICING THE SMALL FOR THE BIG – FOR THE GREATER GOOD."

they release the entire show, it'll all make sense and be looked on probably a little more fondly than it was [at the time it aired] for a lot of folks. I looked at some of the episodes the other day, and there's an interesting storyline that takes place, and I think they had to go where they did in season two in order to get where they're going in season three. [In] season two, they wanted to tell a story in a different way and continually progress in the way that the characters were relating with each other. It was courageous, I think, and in many ways, the tree bore fruit, because they've learned what works and what worked less. I think it was a very informative thing that happened, the way it all unfolded in season two. It wasn't the same formula. In season one, we had a definitive goal – 'save the cheerleader, save the world.' Season two didn't, at the outset, have such a definable goal."

Things didn't look too good for Nathan at the end of season two – but is the character actually dead? Naturally, Pasdar isn't allowed to say,

but he conceded, "I think the idea that two bullets to the chest could take down a guy like Nathan Petrelli is very interesting. I think if they want to turn this into a 'Who shot J.R.?,' that would be fine. I said, 'If you think that's going to do it, after he's come through

the troposphere burning up, after flying through space with his brother…'"

What does Pasdar think of the public's reaction to *Heroes*? "I think it's a great experience for the viewers, just like it is for us. It's been a great way to contribute to the landscape of TV. I think, overall, we've had a pretty positive impact domestically, and internationally too, I know. It's been an incredible ride. We were just all on this European world tour – Milo, Hayden, myself and Jack [Coleman, who plays Noah Bennet] – and it was mind-blowing the reception that we got in every country we went to. There were thousands of people coming out for us. It was really exciting. We were like The Beatles for about five minutes. It's a little scary when you have 8,000 people lining the streets, and you have maybe 200 cops. It's fun, it's great, it's exciting, it's just some people are probably built better for that than I am – I'm kind of a quiet guy, it was a little overwhelming. But certainly, it was an experience that very few people ever get in their lives and that wasn't lost on me. I felt grateful and I was very happy for all that support." ☼

Above: Nathan sees his burned self in season two; This pic: Nathan and Matt Parkman search for answers in season two

THOUGHT POLICE

Matt Parkman is the perfect example of a typical *Heroes* character. He's an everyday guy with the kind of problems that beset any normal person – except that he has to get to grips with a set of super-human powers on top of all this. Actor **Greg Grunberg** talks about the fan-favorite character...

This pic: Matt Parkman at work; Right: Matt confronts his evil dad Maury...

Matt Parkman has had it rough. He loses his job as an LAPD officer because his co-workers believe his psychic powers are a sign of mental instability, he loses his wife after he finds out she's pregnant by someone else, and he finds out that his long-lost father is the "Nightmare Man." However, all this has been great news for actor Greg Grunberg, who's enjoying the challenge of playing the trouble-prone telepath.

"I'm floating. Absolutely floating," he enthuses. "*Heroes* has caught on like a wildfire and it's just great to be a part of it."

Born in Los Angeles, Grunberg has done a lot of work for longtime friend J.J. Abrams, first as a series regular in Abrams' college dramedy *Felicity,* and then in five seasons of Abrams' spy thriller *Alias,* as good-hearted C.I.A. agent Eric Weiss (he also appeared as the ill-fated pilot in Abrams' *Lost,* and had a cameo in the Abrams-directed *Mission: Impossible III*). Other credits include the feature films *Hollow Man, Austin Powers in Goldmember,* and *The Ladykillers. Heroes* came along shortly after *Alias* ended, but it wasn't initially what Grunberg thought he'd be doing. "There was sort of a double wrap-up [with Abrams], and I had developed and shot a pilot for ABC, *The Catch.* I thought it turned out fantastic. It was me and Don Rickles. It didn't get picked up, so it was kind of disappointing. When that didn't happen, I got a call [saying that] they were doing another sitcom pilot at NBC. That didn't get picked up either. I'm just really lucky that the networks continue to feel that I can carry a show. But I always want to surround myself with

> "THERE'S SO MUCH TO DO ON THIS SHOW – YEARS AND YEARS AND YEARS' WORTH, I HOPE!"

unbelievable people. Or be one of those unbelievable people with someone else in someone else's show. I just want to do good work.

"If anybody was looking for a series, it was me – I was ready to do something bigger and have more of a prominent role in the show [than on *Alias*], although I loved being part of a great ensemble. They sent me the [*Heroes* pilot] script. I read it and it immediately felt like something that J.J. or [*Alias* staff writer/producer] Jesse [Alexander] or [*Lost* co-creator] Damon [Lindelof] would have written. A show is the most interesting to me when questions are asked within the story. *Heroes* just felt like it had a life that could go on forever."

Originally, Grunberg read for the role of Peter Petrelli, but once they'd met, Kring found he envisioned the actor as Matt. "He was really looking for an Everyman," Grunberg explains, "a character who everybody could relate to, someone sympathetic and strong. And then [*Heroes* pilot director and long-time Grunberg friend] Dave Semel calls me and says, 'We're messengering over a copy of the two-hour script to your house right now. You have to read it – you'd be great in this role. Tim really, really hopes you connect with it.' I read it and I thought it was my favorite character of all the characters. So I immediately called my agent and they called NBC and said, 'If you guys want me, I'd love to do this.' And that's the way it happened."

Did Grunberg do any research into the psychic and/or police officer aspects of Matt's persona? "Ed Cranes, one of the chief detectives in the Beverly Hills Police Department, is a friend of mine, and I did a ride-along with them, which was unbelievable! Not much happened on my

This pic: Matt investigates the death of Kaito Nakamura

first ride-along, it was just during the day, but I found that more educational than anything else. My character on the show [started out] very unsatisfied with where he was. He wanted more action, he wanted to be on the SWAT team, but he's got dyslexia and he couldn't pass the test. I wanted to get that sort of [quality] where Matt's job is just second nature, it's not anything that's a big deal. To someone who's not a cop, they might feel [about situations the police encounter], 'Oh, my God, this is going to be so exciting!' But it's just something that [police] deal with every day.

"Because of *Alias*, I'm very comfortable with a gun and I'm very comfortable with the stunts and the action and putting on tactical gear and [getting to where] it just feels right and not, 'Eh, it's uncomfortable in that uniform.' It takes it to a different level when you're playing a beat cop, because you've got all sorts of gear. It's like 25, 30 pounds' worth of [clothing]. There's the flak jacket that's under the uniform, and the gun and this and that and the radio – I don't know how those guys outrun anyone," he laughs. "It's an aerobic workout [just] walking down the street in all that gear, but I got used to it and I loved it."

Working on the two Abrams series has helped with working on *Heroes*, Grunberg notes. "I've sort of prepared for this unknowingly. I mean, *Felicity* was a character drama and it was all about those quiet character moments in relationships and dealing with character. *Alias* was carrying a gun and going from zero to the end of the world in two seconds,

COMIC MATT

There are quite a few comic book and cartoon images of the *Heroes* characters, and Grunberg is often bemused by how Matt is depicted in this medium. "It's sort of like my 'before' picture," he laughs. "I lost 25 pounds and these comic book images – I thought the camera was supposed to add 10 pounds – but the pen adds 30 pounds! But I've been in *Mad Magazine* twice – once for *Alias* and once for *Felicity* – and I think it's the ultimate form of flattery."

and this is a combination of both. So it doesn't scare me, it's not overwhelming – it's exciting to do."

At the beginning, Grunberg says Matt's attitude was one of confusion. "When [Matt] realized [that he was hearing other people's thoughts], he tried to figure out where they were coming from. He hadn't even begun to think about controlling it. He was definitely confused and making sure that he wasn't going crazy. I think that's the way I would handle it if all of a sudden I started hearing thoughts. I would be like, 'What the hell – where is that coming from?'"

At the end of season one, things didn't look so good for Matt, with four bullets in his chest. Did Grunberg know that the character would be back for season two? "They didn't have a cliffhanger for me and then Tim Kring called and said, 'You know what? I really love your character, and it's too important and I don't want it to just sit there. I don't want to just have this moment where you're in the square and all this stuff happens and you don't have a part of it. So,' he said, 'you go after Sylar, and we're going to do something with it, and trust me, everything will be okay.' That's all he said. And then I got the script and I get shot four times. But where does that leave me? They hadn't worked out the second season, and I didn't know if there was going to be a flashback, I didn't know if I was going to survive. I love these guys, I really do. But you never know. Story is story, characters are characters – they've got to do what they've got to do. So I'm very happy with the way it turned out."

Like many *Heroes* fans, Grunberg is excited about the special features on the DVD box-sets. For season one, he says, "They were following all our behind-the-scenes people, which is actually very cool. We have some really interesting characters, as every office does. We've got a really good family of people on our crew. There were people last year who went off and did some other great things; it's been a launching pad for people on the crew and cast. But there are some interesting characters. I think people will enjoy that."

A lot of Grunberg's time in the past year has been spent on *Group Sex* – that's the title of an independent film, not a real-life activity, we hasten to add! Grunberg relates, "I wrote it with Lawrence Trilling, who [was a show-runner on] *Alias* and ran *Invasion* with Shaun Cassidy. He's a very good friend of mine – we wrote a romantic comedy and we actually got

This pic: The Matt in the mirror; Right: Evil Future Matt interrogates Hiro; Below Right: Matt with his ward, Molly; Below: Matt interrogates Angela Petrelli

"THEY SENT ME THE [HEROES PILOT] SCRIPT. IT JUST FELT LIKE IT HAD A LIFE THAT COULD GO ON FOREVER."

the funding for it." Grunberg and Trilling are two of the film's producers. "It's going to be great. I'm starring in it and Larry's directing it."

An ongoing project close to Grunberg's heart is the rock-and-roll outfit Band From TV, which raises money for various charities. Grunberg is particularly interested in helping organizations that support research and treatment for epilepsy, as one of his three sons is affected by the condition. "We have a website, *BandFromTV.net*. It's me and Hugh Laurie and James Denton and Bonnie Sommerville and Lucy Lawless and all these great people in the band. [The popularity of *Heroes*] just adds to the credibility and the recognition and it makes it more exciting for people to come out and see us and that just generates more money for the charities, which is great. It helps me to try and remove the stigma that's attached to epilepsy, so I love that."

Matt has mostly been a good guy on *Heroes*, but there are suggestions he could follow in his father's mind-manipulating footsteps, and in the speculative

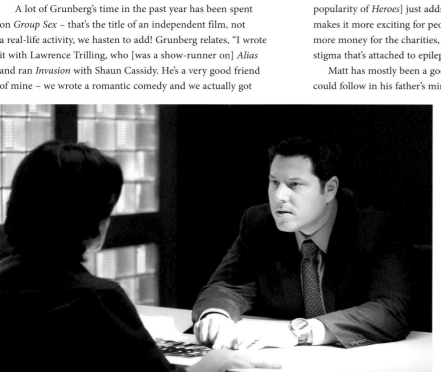

future episode *Five Years Gone*, he is, as Grunberg describes him, "A badass dude. I think what's really cool about that is, all these characters get to a crossroads and they'll continue to do that, where they can use their powers for good or evil. And not that it was justified, that I was going around killing all these characters, but I thought I was doing the right thing – I didn't know I was working for Sylar. Parkman thought he was working for the President, and it turned out to be Sylar. He was protecting his family and didn't want them to be located."

Grunberg has had at least one more badass role, starring as a serial killer opposite Band From TV colleague Lawless in the horror thriller *Darkroom*. "My character is a very, very evil guy, probably one of the worst characters I could ever play. I loved working with those guys, [producer] Mark Altman and all the people at his company,

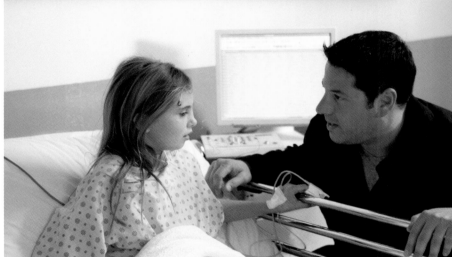

they were pros. It's something you'd never cast me in off the bat. I think it was a really interesting bit of casting. I said, 'Look, I'm not going to sit here and sell myself to you, but I think it would be so great to cast me as a bad guy, because you're not going to expect it.' That was always one of the things I selfishly wanted: at the very end of *Alias*, [the villain] Sloane goes in somewhere and he's talking to his superior and you realize it's me – how crazy would that be?" Grunberg laughs. It would have been like, 'What? Weiss is behind everything?' I was everyone's confidant. Yes, the guy who loves calzones also loves making bombs! I always said [to Abrams], 'You've got to make me evil!' I actually told him early, like in the second year, that I'd love to go undercover following the head of a mob organization, some guy who's getting into weapons somehow and I would ingratiate myself into his family and his group. And then of course I'm attracted by that and possibly doing

> "ALL OF THESE ABILITIES, THEY COME TO JUST REGULAR PEOPLE, WHO ARE DEALING WITH CRAZY, EVERYDAY STUFF IN THEIR LIVES, JUST TRYING TO SURVIVE. I JUST THINK THAT THERE ARE SO MANY INTERESTING WAYS TO GO."

some things I shouldn't be doing... But [Abrams] didn't love the idea, because it took me out of the C.I.A. and it took me out of where we were. I always thought that would really be a great thing for me to do!"

Grunberg is happy to expound on all things *Heroes*. "Tim Kring has taken this subject and he's really humanized it. [Before the series began airing] I told people what I was doing. They were like, 'Oh, like X-Men!' And I said, 'No, I don't open up my closet and there are tights and a cape hanging. All of these abilities come to just regular people, who are dealing with crazy, everyday stuff in their lives, just trying to survive, just trying to do what they do.' I just think that there are so many interesting ways to go. The great balance of the show is that you've got this visually stimulating stuff, like a cheerleader falling off of an oil-rig and smashing down and cracking her bone back into place, so visually, you're [thinking], 'Wow, that's great.' But the majority of the time, you're dealing with these people, and [the question] of what would you actually do if you woke up in the morning and you stepped out of bed and your foot levitated off the floor? It's not like, 'Oh, it's the coolest fantasy I've ever had – flying through the air!' It comes with a lot of baggage and secrets and trouble will follow you. It's really, really interesting. I think that they've really got a good formula and a good tone to this. And then of course, we've got the dark element of the show – the evil force trying to stop all of us from fully developing our skills, our abilities, our coming together to save the world. So there's so much to do on this show – years and years and years' worth, I hope!" he concludes. ↻

The Astonishing

FX-Men

Can you believe a man can fly? A cheerleader can survive any injury? Or a girl can throw electricity? Well, actually you can, thanks to Stargate Digital, the superhuman team who create the visual effects on *Heroes.*

Heroes visual effects supervisor, Eric Grenaudier, and Stargate Digital's supervising producer, Mark Spatny, talk about how the *Heroes* actors travel without leaving the studio, creating a CG doppelganger for Claire, and why they can't wait for Sylar to turn frosty...

Nathan Petrelli can fly fast enough to break the sound barrier, Claire Bennet can recover from seemingly fatal wounds, and Sylar can send thousands of shards of broken glass sailing across a room. However, none of these superpowers would look like any great shakes without the sterling work of Stargate Digital, the company that does all of *Heroes'* computer-generated imagery, better known, of course, as CGI.

Stargate, which also does effects for a wide variety of other series, including *Reaper* and *Dirty Sexy Money* (but not, ironically, considering their name, for the *Stargate* series), is located in Pasadena, California. In one area of their studio, a team of 3D animators all work on creating individual elements for special effects shots in their computers. Compositors work at other computers, matching the CG elements to live-action, or "practical," elements. Meanwhile, upstairs is the video library, where Stargate's archivists are able to pull in a wide variety of shots of New York, Tokyo, and pretty much any other place where *Heroes* sets its globe-trotting storylines.

(Continues overleaf...)

"I'M LOOKING FORWARD TO DOING SYLAR'S FREEZING POWER AT SOME POINT, BECAUSE WE'VE NEVER ACTUALLY SEEN IT."

Previous spread: Top:
Nathan looks over
a devastated New York;
Bottom: Claire's season
two leap from the
Hollywood sign; Ted's
nuclear powers; New
York gets blown up...
This spread:
More New York
destruction;
Top right: Peter is
set to explode...
Right: Sylar tidies
Mohinder's apartment...
Below: Elle gets
a taste of her own
electrical medicine

FINAL CUT

When Sylar telekinetically throws a shower of flying glass at Peter Petrelli in season one, the effect is created digitally, as it's not possible to do physically (at least, not without injuring the actors...).

On the computer, the glass shards are initially represented by black 2D shapes. CGI artist Mike Cook explains, "What they do on set is, they take a multitude of images [of the room itself] in a 360-degree view and we can use the images to put accurate lighting onto the 3D objects."

"There was a real shard that was in the episode, so we wanted to make it look the same," adds fellow CGI practitioner Ryan Weaver.

"The props department originally made a bunch of different pieces of broken glass," Mark Spatny relates, "and said, 'Pick one. How big is it? Is it jagged, is it triangular?' Eventually [the producers] settled on one. By rebuilding the room in [the computer in] 3D, you'll actually see the room reflected in the pieces of glass."

"The first thing we would do is put 20 or 30 shards of glass up in the air [as] flat pictures [in the computer]," Eric Granaudier reveals. "We animate them. [Then the film editors] might say, 'We think it should be twice as big,' or 'It should be a third of that size.' We'll refine those parameters, and once we have a pretty good concept of the size of the shards, the number of shards, and the speed at which they could be traveling, then we'll produce the shot. When somebody says, 'We want Sylar to break a window, have glass come up off the ground, levitate for awhile and then be thrown at a given character,' there are a lot of subjective [opinions] as to how that should happen. It opens the door to a lot of conversations among us. The final touch of the glass – the lighting, the texture, the transparency – would be the last thing we would do."

SCREEN BURN

Mark Spatny is particularly proud of the sequence where Claire heals as she emerges from her burning house in *Company Man*. "Originally, the plan was to have various photo doubles [for Hayden Panettiere] in stages of make-up that they would cut between. On the day of shooting, it became evident that that wasn't going to work, because although the actresses *looked* like Claire, they didn't *perform* like Claire. They didn't have Hayden's way of walking. So we created a CG double and exactly matched it to [Panettiere's] performance and then [went between the live actress and the CG character]. Eric [Grenaudier] had a lot to do with that, as the artist who put all the elements together. Our 3D artist had to create a CG version of her and frame by frame match the position of her body – so he'd bring up a frame, line it up, get the hands and the fingers and the face and the body and the shoulders all correct, and then build the next frame and do it again."

Mark Spatny is the supervising producer at Stargate Digital, and Eric Grenaudier is the visual effects supervisor for *Heroes* itself. Strangely, however, neither of them imagined they'd wind up in their current field.

"I initially thought that I was going to be an astronaut," Spatny laughs. "I worked really hard through high school with that goal in mind, and then I discovered I needed glasses and so I was no longer qualified to be a pilot." He wound up studying aerospace engineering, then got into set and lighting design. With that combination, it just "seemed natural to go into computer graphics."

Grenaudier, meanwhile, says he took an even more unconventional route. "I actually studied micro-economics and political science in France [where he grew up]. I was going to go into politics or diplomacy." However, he wound up in Los Angeles, working as a production assistant. "So the years I spent at university have been of absolutely no use..."

So how exactly does the world of visual effects operate? "A lot of [the episodes] will have at least three meetings," Spatny adds. "There's a concept meeting where the writers and the executive producers get together with all the key depart-ment heads and say, 'This is our idea of what we'd really like to happen in this episode.' And the department heads – [including] us,

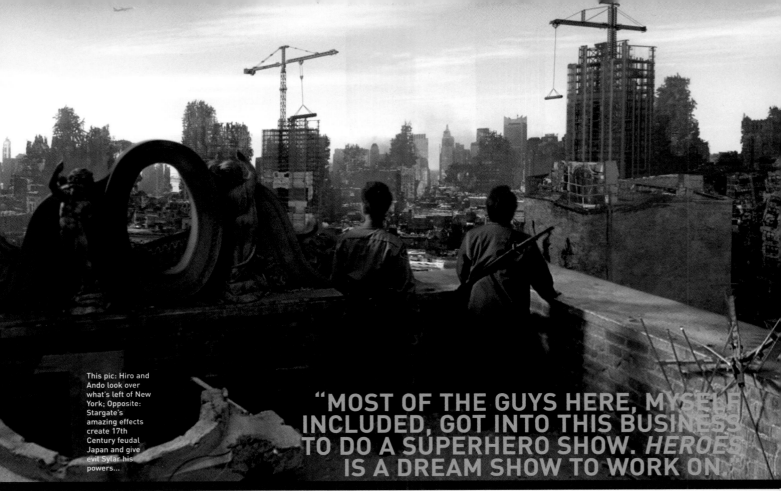

This pic: Hiro and Ando look over what's left of New York; Opposite: Stargate's amazing effects create 17th Century feudal Japan and give evil Sylar his powers...

"MOST OF THE GUYS HERE, MYSELF INCLUDED, GOT INTO THIS BUSINESS TO DO A SUPERHERO SHOW. *HEROES* IS A DREAM SHOW TO WORK ON."

transportation, production design – figure out what it's going to take to do it. Then individual meetings happen. So we'll have a visual effects meeting where we sit down with the director of the episode and go through the exact parameters of how we're going to shoot stuff, what we're going to need, what departments we're going to need to work with. Then we get another big meeting with all the department heads, where we all talk about everything we've figured out in the past week that we need to work with each other on.'

Often, the Stargate Digital people create *Heroes*' visual effects in collaboration with the practical special make-up effects team at Optic Nerve. "They do remarkable work," Grenaudier says. "Quite often, there will be shots where one cut of the shot is using a prosthetic, the next cut is using the CG version of that same effect, and vice-versa. When we did Nathan's face with the burns [as Peter and Nathan are flying away from the explosion, and when Nathan is manipulated by Maury Parkman], some elements were prosthetic, some elements were fully CG elements, some of them were a bit of both. [That kind of thing] happens a lot. And the more technicians you have in the departments, the more we can help each other."

So how do the team create effects on the human body? Daniel Kumiega explains that the

HIGH FLYERS

The *Heroes* actors often talk about being filmed high up on wires for flying scenes. If they're being photographed against green screens, why does it matter whether they're off the ground at all?

"When you have an extensive array of green screens, because light bounces off surfaces, that green light will actually spill on [the actors]," Eric Grenaudier explains. "So if you can have some separation between them and the green surface, it's not a bad thing. More importantly, a lot of the shots we're trying to achieve are a combination of movement on their part and movement on the part of the camera. They [need to be] 10 or 12 feet off the ground, so the camera can swoop. So we need space for the camera to move around."

"One thing that we've learned," Mark Spatny adds, "is that any time you see a flying character who's static, your eye instantly recognizes there's something wrong. But if you keep the camera moving and do dynamic things around [the character], it becomes more realistic."

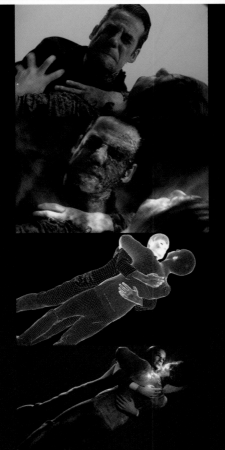

This pic: D.L.'s Stargate-aided powers; Below: Green-screen helps create Hollywood, a future vision, and Hiro's office

grid in the shape of a human body on his computer screen is called a "wire frame." Moving individual lines of the frame will affect the head, arm, and leg movements of the 3D representation of the character.

Sometimes shots require a more unconventional approach, such as when characters like D.L. or Peter walk through walls. "Well, we have very talented artists who say to themselves, 'What would concrete look like from the inside?'"

Spatny chuckles. "It wouldn't look like anything, because there'd be no light. So we're making up what somebody's perception of what the inside of a concrete wall is."

"A lot of it is going to have to be done by [the actor on set], entering the space that should be divided by the wall that is obviously not there," Grenaudier elaborates. "One way of helping with visually marking where the wall would be is to create shafts of light or shadows on the plane of

where the wall would be. So suddenly, as the actor is entering the concrete wall, the lighting on that portion of the space or its profile will be changing, which gives us a demarcation line of where it is. In the computer, the 3D artists will build a 3D wall that exists in space where it should be. The compositors will take the image of the actor walking into empty space, which in most cases will be shot green screen. So now we have a cut-out of this person, and as he's coming

ALL AROUND THE WORLD

Whether a far-off location utilizes actual footage or just a matte painting depends on how often and how much we'll see it, Mark Spatny says. "In season two, Mohinder has a meeting in Cairo and [the producers] wanted to see Cairo out the window. We can create that with just a matte. We'll get some photographic elements and put it together.

"If it's a specific location that we know we're going to be in a lot, we will send a unit out on location. For *Heroes*, we've sent camera crews to New York twice to shoot locations. We can put people in moving footage, or we'll use footage to create environments. Sometimes we'll use still frames from video and create New York buildings in the background. We'll shoot locations from every conceivable angle, and we'll work with the directors and say, 'Here's how you need to shoot the scene in order to work with the footage.' We shoot wide angles, we shoot narrow angles, we shoot pieces that will be stitched together so that we can create moving camera angles, so that if we want to spin the camera around the person or pan off to reveal something, we can do that."

through the space where the wall would be, by looking at the change of lighting on his face, we can almost do a cut-out of the edges that are being progressively [altered by the light] frame by frame. At this point, it's live-action flat on the piece of film, so we can judge where the tip of the nose of the actor is, now where the wall would be."

Grenaudier feels the most challenging effects he's done so far as a supervisor were in the sequence with Peter and Nathan after the explosion above New York. "It was challenging just because of the scale of it and the complexity of the shot, having to apply the burn texture on the moving character of Nathan within camera."

The Stargate team are always up for new challenges. Spatny says, "I'm looking forward

"THE LEVEL OF EXPECTATION ON THIS SHOW IS EXTREMELY HIGH. USUALLY FEATURE FILMS WILL HAVE SIX MONTHS TO A YEAR TO DO BIG VISUAL EFFECTS. WE WILL HAVE SIX TO TEN *DAYS*."

to doing Sylar's freezing power at some point, because we've never actually seen it. We've seen the aftermath, where there's a house with frozen bodies, and we've had one or two shots in an episode where we actually saw his hand turn to ice and give off vapor, but we've only teased it."

"The level of expectation on this show is extremely high," Grenaudier observes. "Usually feature films will have six months to a year to do big visual effects. We will have six to ten *days*. That's the tricky part. It's hard to be consistently at the highest level of quality with a tight schedule."

Spatny notes, "We do a lot of things for bread and butter, where we put New York behind somebody for one episode of some [other] show. That's great, and that pays the bills. But I think most of the guys here, myself included, got into this business to do a superhero show. *Heroes* is a dream show to work on."

She's Electric

Season two of *Heroes* saw the introduction of several new faces to the cast, and Kristen Bell's character Elle certainly made a big impact. As the slightly unhinged daughter of Company leader Bob, she kept audience members and the Heroes themselves on their toes...
The popular actress reveals more about electric Elle...

It's hard to imagine anyone playing *Heroes*' lively, laboratory-raised, lightning-throwing, deeply conflicted character other than Kristen Bell. Perhaps this is because the evolution of Elle has been heavily influenced by the actress. As *Heroes* creator/executive producer Tim Kring explains: "When you cast an actor with as much personality as Kristen has, we try to tailor the character a little closer to the actress."

Michigan-born Bell studied acting in school and was soon performing theatre professionally. She made her Broadway debut in 2001 as Becky Thatcher in the musical *The Adventures of Tom Sawyer* and went on to appear with Laura Linney and Liam Neeson in the 2002 revival of Arthur Miller's drama *The Crucible*. Her first onscreen role was in the TV series *The O'Keefes*. On the big screen, Bell's credits include David Mamet's *Spartan*, the horror thriller *The Pulse*, the title role in the new comedy *Forgetting Sarah Marshall*, and as one of the leads in the upcoming *Fanboys*. On TV, Bell has racked up an impressive number of guest and recurring roles in just a few years, including a turn as a young prostitute on HBO's *Deadwood*; concurrent with *Heroes*, she's the heard-but-not-seen voice of the narrator on The CW's *Gossip Girl*. However, prior to *Heroes*, Bell was best known and beloved for her three years starring as UPN's teenage sleuth *Veronica Mars*. The last season of *Veronica* overlapped with the first season of *Heroes*, which was a favorite topic of conversation on the set, according to Bell.

"I'm a huge fan of [*Heroes*]," Bell reveals. "I watched it from the first episode and I joked with the writers that *Heroes* was the water-cooler conversation at *Veronica Mars* on set. I put feelers out there at Comic-Con and let them know what a fan I was of the show, I think with the secret hope that one day I could be a part of it..."

What's most exciting about *Heroes* for you?
KRISTEN BELL: When I caught the [first] season premiere, it was just so engulfing that I couldn't think about anything else. I'm not kidding when I say it was the water-cooler conversation when we were working on *Veronica Mars*. We would come to work and the entire camera crew was standing around and would be like, 'Did you see what happened last night? And did you see who Claire's father is?' There are hooks that people are able to sink into you when telling a story that I think Tim [Kring] has mastered and I think [*Veronica Mars* creator] Rob Thomas mastered for the much smaller but certainly avid [audience] that we had on *Veronica Mars*. It makes you want to be involved. I think also they're really smart shows and they're a little harder to follow, which I really respect, because when you credit the audience with intelligence, you tend to attract intelligent viewers.

The medium for me is the difference. I certainly love and miss theatre. Film is so much fun as well, and it's a little bit more like camp, because you're usually on location and you have a couple of months of time with people that you get really close with and then it's sort of like end-of-the-summer syndrome. With TV, I really like the security and I like the sense of family. I like knowing who I work with. I work in this business because I like performing and I also really like the creative relationships. And I think coming forth with people that

"HEROES WAS THE WATER-COOLER CONVERSATION WHEN WE WERE WORKING ON VERONICA MARS. WE WOULD COME TO WORK AND WOULD BE LIKE, 'DID YOU SEE WHAT HAPPENED LAST NIGHT? AND DID YOU SEE WHO CLAIRE'S FATHER IS?'"

you love and being able to see them on a daily basis is a really special thing. Not that many people get to absolutely love what they do, and I'm lucky to be one of those people.

Was it intimidating for you to join a cast that had already been working together for a season?
There was anxiety and nerves, certainly, but nothing about it has been hard. They are some of the nicest people I've really ever worked with, and having had social relationships with a few of them, I'd heard through the grapevine what a great job it was. It's not just an excellent show, it's really fun to be a part of an ensemble that really supports each other. I think to find all that in one setting is very hard. Clearly, that says a lot about what comes down through the grapevine, starting with Tim Kring. Every time you join a different job or a different show, I feel it's kind of like changing schools. It's that anxiety of, "Is everyone going to like me? Is this going to be fun? Am I going to do well?" And the warmth that I was greeted with, it felt like I was starting a school that all my friends already went to.

In some ways, that's a pretty exact analogy. You've known some of your *Heroes* cast-mates off-screen for years already...

Yeah (*laughs*). I have known Hayden Panettiere [Claire Bennet] since she was eight – we met in New York. We have the same agent. I was just then in college and met her in some plays that I did in New York. She was a lovely little girl. Even then, at eight years old, you could tell that there was something so alarmingly special about who she was and what she was going to be able to accomplish as a performer. I kept up a relationship with her, just socially, and having joined the cast now, it's been really nice, because I think really good girlfriends are so rare to find in L.A. She's a really cool, honest girl, and so we've become closer through the show. We always used to joke about trying to play sisters or friends in a project, and we might not be either of those in this show, but it's still fun to get to work together.

Geek Girl?
Kristen Bell on her nerdy side...

"I think Comic-Con is my geeky guilty pleasure. I think the geekiest of all my pleasure at Comic-Con is I definitely try to get pictures with every single person who dresses up, because the people who come in full costume absolutely fascinate me. Having done *Fanboys*, anything *Star Wars* is now wonderful and fascinating to me. I'm still learning about it all. And all my friends are fanboys, so I'm learning about it all from them. I've just been so embraced by this community that I love it. Now I'm sort of coming into my own as a fangirl and seeking things out, like in Los Angeles, they had a double bill of *Tron* and *The Last Starfighter*. I just thought, 'I want to see that at least once in my life...'"

Fanboys photo © MGM

Zachary Quinto [Sylar] has been a good friend of mine for almost 10 years now and I've always wanted to work with him. [As Sylar] he's pretty much the coolest thing, because he's so unpredictable and so downright evil. It's almost hard for me to watch, because it's the polar opposite of Zach's personality, because he's just the kindest, gentlest, most giving person. I would love to see him and Elle face off properly one day – I think that that would be unbelievable.

What was it like going from playing the heroic Veronica to the morally-muddled Elle?

(*Laughs*) It is so much fun. I have always played about 10 years younger than I am, which is a major blessing, even in real life. My family's very petite and I have a young-looking face, I guess, so I'm thankful to my parents for good genes! That being said, as an actor, there are certain things that I'm going for in my own life, in my late 20s, things I'm experiencing, and that's what you draw upon in your acting, so I hope that I'll be accepted as playing closer to my age. I still look a lot younger, but I'm thankful just to be out of "teenage girl" a little bit. I don't dislike it at all – I've just had a lot of it.

I'd been crossing my fingers in the hopes that I could get a job soon where I could play someone who was – I like to call it "a little off" – [who] perhaps didn't have the brightest and shiniest of intentions, and this character is so conflicted and comes across as such a risk. It's so much fun to play that. Elle doesn't have many boundaries, which I think is the really interesting part of playing this character on this particular show, because the whole first season has been about very good-natured people trying to embrace these abilities and being very conflicted as to how they should use them. Elle is not that way at all. She very much enjoys her power and enjoys the emotional power it gives her over other people. [Elle has] determination and she has a very fierce and intense personality. When she wants something, she wants it and she wants it now, which I think is good when you're working with the good guys and it's really bad when you're working with the bad guys. I think that's what she'll kind of ping-pong between. She has an inability to decipher between right and wrong. That's what makes her so interesting. She always thinks what she's doing is right, but she was raised by The Company and not by a normal family. I certainly hope you'll sympathize with her in trying to understand how her childhood really messed her up, and then hopefully she'll get a little bit of redemption.

Do your fans from *Veronica Mars* accept you as Elle? Do you interact with your fans?
Well, one thing I will say about *Veronica Mars* fans – whether it's on a street corner or whether it's on a blog, they're definitely interactive. It's a little deeper character work when you have to really figure out someone's intentions, because I don't think even evil characters are evil. They always think they're doing something right, and it's to get to that sort of conflicted "what's the difference between right and wrong?" point,

"THE *HEROES* CAST ARE SOME OF THE NICEST PEOPLE I'VE REALLY EVER WORKED WITH. IT'S AN ENSEMBLE THAT REALLY SUPPORTS EACH OTHER."

which is fun and cool to work on as an actor. I hope everybody's going to have fun with it, because I love rooting for the underdog, but it's also fun to play someone who's a little crazy.

The *Heroes* cast reportedly is often almost as in the dark as the audience about what's coming next. Is it hard to play a character when you don't know what the scenes are building towards?
That was one thing on the first season of *Veronica Mars* that we struggled with a lot – all of the actors – and I've come to the conclusion that it's all about trust. I mean it when I say it – I was really lucky that when I was pitched the character [of Elle], Tim Kring let a few facts out of the bag, which was exciting and certainly something that I would never repeat. But ultimately, I think, when you're working on a show that's centered around a mystery, it's of vital importance that you have to trust [that the writers will] let the actor know what they need to know – what should I be showing, as far as being able to tell the story adequately and foreshadowing, and things like that. You just have to trust your creator and your writers and your director that if you weren't giving enough, or they needed to allude to something, they would tell you. It's just got to be all about trust.

Do people ask you for *Heroes* spoilers?
Yeah, of course! Even among the cast, everybody's always asking everybody else who has more information. When I started on *Heroes*, I would just go around with a big old smile on my face (*laughs*), so maybe they could sense it... But I had a substantial amount of information and all the other cast-members were sort of trying to pick it out of me. But I think I do a pretty good job of just smiling through it and just knowing that

Kristen Bell
Selected Credits

Kristen Bell shot to fame playing the title role in *Veronica Mars* and since then her career has sky-rocketed, with movie roles and TV appearances... Let's take a look at how she got there, and what she's done since.

TV

Gossip Girl (2007-present) – Gossip Girl (Voice)
Heroes (2007-2008) – Elle Bishop
Veronica Mars (2004-2007) – Veronica Mars
Deadwood (2004) – Flora Anderson
Everwood (2003) – Stacey Wilson
The O'Keefes (2003) – Virginia's Owner
American Dreams (2003) – Amy Fielding
The Shield (2003) – Jessica Hintel

MOVIES

Forgetting Sarah Marshall (2008) – Sarah Marshall
Flatland: The Movie (2007) – Hex
Roman (2006) – The Girl
Pulse (2006) – Mattie
Fifty Pills (2006) – Gracie
The Receipt (2005) – Pretty Girl
Deepwater (2005) – Nurse Laurie
Reefer Madness: The Movie Musical (2005) – Mary Lane
Spartan (2004) – Laura Newton
Pootie Tang (2001) – Record Executive's Daughter

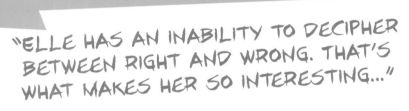

"ELLE HAS AN INABILITY TO DECIPHER BETWEEN RIGHT AND WRONG. THAT'S WHAT MAKES HER SO INTERESTING..."

I was lucky enough to be told a little bit where my character was going, to at least know her first arc. And you know, it's hard, because when you have secrets, of course you want to spill them, but you have to realize how vital it is to keep them secret and that it's actually kind of fun when you know a little bit more information than everyone else.

Do your former *Veronica Mars* cast-mates ask for spoilers?
Oh my god. Every single one of them. I was having breakfast with Ryan Hansen [who played Ted Casablancas], and he of course was asking questions. Also, the [*Veronica Mars*] crew watched *Heroes*, so I would get a lot of texts. I kind of like to hold it over their heads, I'm not going to lie to you! I'm like, "Why don't you just watch?" and they're like, "Auggh, Kristen!" (*laughs*)

Between *Heroes* and *Veronica Mars*, you've become something of a pop culture icon…
The thing about pop culture for me is that I would so much rather be on a show that people are wildly obsessed with than on a show that people just turn on because it's on prime-time television. As a performer and as a creative person on a TV show, you want people to invest in your project. You want people to love it, not just like it. And as far as the coolest fans ever, which are some of the ones I've run into – I mean, it can get really intense, I'm not going to lie. The one thing that is different about those kind of fans – because they are *so* invested – more times than not, when they see you, they don't really know what to do with themselves. It's not just, "Oh, that's a person I watch on a television show," it's, "That's the person I follow and am deeply invested in." There's a lot of shaking and sweaty palms and tears, but it's precious. They're all kind of funny and bizarre, but at the same time they're lovely, because they're coming up to you because they support you.

How did you get to be so cool?
(*Laughs*) Oh, my goodness. I don't think I'm that cool. I just try to be nice and enjoy what I'm doing. I've been really lucky and I feel grateful for that every moment and I hope that comes across, because I love what I do and I want to keep doing it. You know what? I have the coolest friends ever. That's how I'm cool!

COMPANY MAN

Considering he hasn't got any powers, it's a miracle that Noah Bennet has survived his time on *Heroes* so far (although he did have a bit of help from Claire's healing blood).
The busy actor shares his thoughts on Mr. Horn-Rimmed Glasses...

Picture this: *Heroes*' Noah Bennet belting out 'Greased Lightning' (from the musical *Grease*). This is how Jack Coleman, who plays Bennet, got started as a professional actor.

"My first love was sports," he explains, "but by the time I was approaching my teens, I realized I was not going to be a professional basketball player. I don't think I thought of acting as a profession until I was in my senior year in high school/freshman year in college. I auditioned at that time as Danny Zuko in *Grease* on Broadway. I had a million callbacks, didn't get it, finished college, came back, and auditioned for it again right as it was leaving Broadway and going out to this theatre in Long Island. I was so familiar with the part and the audition process at that point that I got it."

Any chance, then, that we'll see H.R.G. singing in the shower? "I don't think Noah Bennet showers," Coleman deadpans. "He has a hyperbaric chamber which he walks through."

We're talking at a Starbucks near Coleman's house. The day is so warm that Coleman's wife, actress Beth Toussaint Coleman, stops by to give her husband a baseball cap so he doesn't get sunburned on his walk home. Coleman notes that the couple met when she guest-starred on an episode of NBC's short-lived supernatural series *Nightmare Cafe*, in which Coleman starred as a soul in limbo. Coleman also appeared on *Days of Our Lives*, and later spent

years as Steven Carrington on ABC's *Dynasty*. Bennet, however, is probably the most challenging ongoing series role the actor has tackled.

Coleman credits his involvement with *Heroes* to several factors. "My friend Daniel Cerone, who's now a show-runner on *Dirty Sexy Money*, was talking about the new crop of pilots [in 2006] and said, 'The one I really like is *Heroes*.' Then it came to me with an audition for the part of 'Man in Horn-Rimmed Glasses' [originally conceived as a recurring character]. Although it wasn't the most auspicious-sounding [character] name, I just loved the mystery of it, the whole idea of playing this shadowy bad guy. I auditioned for it on my birthday.

"Dave Semel, who directed the pilot episode, is somebody I know. I've known [*Heroes* executive producer] Dennis Hammer for years. The casting people, Jason La Padura and Natalie Hart, have hired me a bunch of times. When I found out that I actually got the [part] and I was going to be in the first five episodes, I thought, 'Okay, that's a good sign.' I certainly wasn't thinking 'series regular.' And then right around the fifth or sixth episode, it started to become clear that [because] all the Heroes were just discovering their abilities, there needed to be someone who could paint the bigger picture of what was happening in this world. My character was going to be that guy, and then they really liked Hayden [Panettiere, who plays Bennet's adopted daughter, Claire] and me together, so they just started writing for me more and more."

"I THINK THERE'S A LOT OF REALLY EXCITING STUFF COMING DOWN THE PIKE IN SEASON THREE."

Clockwise from top: Claire Bear is the apple of H.R.G.'s eye (sorry Kyle); H.R.G. pays a visit to Future Claire in *Five Years Gone*; The Haitian and H.R.G. – a force to be reckoned with; West attempts to drag Claire away, as Noah is about to get a nasty injury...

Bennet starts out more nefarious than he becomes as we get to know him. "I think the character was conceived pretty dark," Coleman acknowledges. "Somebody who was hunting these people and bagging and tagging them. While there are certainly some civil rights issues involved here, I think [the writers] were very careful that they didn't make my character too over-the-top villainous. [But] if you look at the first couple of episodes, that's how I played him – a guy who really enjoyed his work. In the second episode, [Claire says], 'You're my dad, and you'll always be my dad,' and we're having a real heart-to-heart. Then she walks away and I'm looking at the tape [that shows Claire's powers]. The audience doesn't know what my intentions are, they just know that I'm the guy who hunts these people and I know that she's one of them. Allan Arkush directed that episode, and he pointed me in the direction right away. After Claire leaves the room, Allan said, 'Let's see the curtain come down. Let's see the loving father go away and the hard-boiled chaser of the special people come back.' In shows like this, you [usually] know within the first minute or so whether someone's a good guy or a bad guy. How do they treat people? What are their intentions? I think Adrian Pasdar's character [Nathan Petrelli] has that kind of slipperiness, too – he's a politician, so you never know what his intentions are. Basically, he loves his brother, but he's also kind of a prick to

his brother," Coleman laughs, "but his brother, Peter, was clearly a Hero. Claire Bennet was clearly a Hero. Hiro Nakamura was clearly a Hero. [Bennet] was very hard to put your finger on."

To get a sense of how he should play certain aspects of Bennet, Coleman asked the writer/producers some questions. "'Did I kill Suresh's father?' The answer was, 'No.' 'Am I C.I.A.?' 'No.' I asked, 'Is my love for my daughter genuine? I'm not just harvesting her?' That was a little more ambiguous, because they definitely wanted that weird thing where they seem like they have this wonderful relationship, but when she walks away, you get a strange sense that maybe he's got a much darker intention for her. I always played that he was a very loving father and I think that dichotomy really worked."

On the other hand, Coleman says he was happy when the series finally de-mystified Bennet's motives to an extent. "At a certain point, you have to come clean with the audience. I was the beneficiary of so many lucky circumstances and so many brilliant decisions by [series creator/executive producer] Tim Kring and the writers to draw it out, but you get to the point where everyone's like, 'Who *is* this guy? It's driving us crazy.' Then I got the episode, *Company Man*, which answered all these questions. I think it came at exactly the right time,

NOT LOST IN TRANSLATION

Contrary to rumor, Coleman *did* know what he was saying in the scenes between H.R.G. and George Takei's Kaito Nakamura in season one's *Company Man*. "I unquestionably learned [the Japanese dialogue] phonetically. But I also knew what I was saying to him and what he was saying back to me. George [who does speak Japanese] was so accommodating and understanding – I had a two-and-a-half-page scene in Japanese. He's just handed baby Claire over to me and it's a big, weighty scene. He was wonderful to work with. Also, I really realized – by working with him – what a wonderful actor he is. When I was saying, 'I don't think I'll be a good father,' and he's saying, 'I'm not asking you; you're taking her, this is what you're doing,' he has tremendous authority."

where the audience had probably had just about as much of the grey, indefinable area as they could deal with. [It addressed] how he came into The Company, how he came into possession of Claire, and that he ultimately is trying to protect her."

Not having superpowers hasn't been a problem. "We've got enough people on our show with powers," Coleman opines. "It's kind of fun being one of the few who doesn't have powers. I think Sendhil [Ramamurthy, who plays Suresh] and I both enjoy not being powered. I like having all the attendant issues that come with being mere flesh and blood amongst all the high-powered Heroes who can do all kinds of things, because I'm more at risk."

How does Coleman feel about *Heroes* season two, which received a mixed critical reaction? "I feel that when people look back on the season, when they're not in as critical a place as they were when it aired, they'll see the mistakes, they'll see that we spent too long on some things, or some things were perhaps not executed as well as they might have been – but the season holds up. There are several really, really strong episodes. It was a growing season for the show, for the writers, for the actors, the directors – it was sort of a necessary step. I think that what you'll see in season three is a return to season one, which is adrenaline and mystery. There are going to be a lot of great story

turns, surprises, and characters popping up in ways and places that you wouldn't expect; very strange bedfellows, uneasy alliances – the kind of thing that *Heroes* does really well. I'm a fairly savvy guy, I'm reading the scripts, I go, 'Oh my God! I never even thought about that!' So I think they've got a lot of really exciting stuff coming down the pike in season three.

"What I've seen so far is, there's more action than there has been, far more than in the first season. I remember people saying that they felt that the first few episodes of the first season

"PETER, CLAIRE BENNET, AND HIRO ARE CLEARLY HEROES. BENNET IS VERY HARD TO PUT YOUR FINGER ON..."

were a little bit slow, even though there was always a great cliffhanger. These [season three episodes] move like a bat out of hell!"

Cristine Rose, who plays Angela Petrelli, has been made a series regular this year, which delights Coleman. "She's fabulous. And she's been around a long time, she's got a lot of credits, it's just really nice to see someone like that rewarded."

Might there be confrontations brewing between H.R.G. and Angela? "I think it's very possible. I'm not speaking from any knowledge, but we have Claire in common, as well as the history in The Company. I'm also hoping that you'll see some sort of custodial issues [over Claire] between H.R.G. and Nathan. You've got the biological father and the adoptive father, so there are all kinds of possibilities there."

Besides, obviously, *Company Man*, Coleman cites season two's *Cautionary Tales* as one of his favorite episodes. "I get shot in the eye! I felt that was a really strong episode. The thing that I loved about it was, basically, there were four stories. And they were essentially the same story. It was all fathers and children. You had Elle and Bob, you had Claire and H.R.G., Hiro and his father, and Matt Parkman and his father. I thought Masi was very moving and wonderful in the Hiro scene on the rooftop where [Hiro and his father] know they're saying goodbye to each other. And it had that drive. That's why I'm saying I think in retrospect, if people [watch season two again] they'll see how strong a lot of the episodes are, because there's a lot of stuff they were building up to, like with the paintings. H.R.G. sees these paintings, which presage his death, and Claire is

IT'S A SMALL WORLD

In a coincidence worthy of *Heroes* itself, Jack Coleman has long been friends with Ashley Crow, who plays his *Heroes* wife Sandra, even though they had never worked together before. Coleman *had* worked with Crow's real-life husband, Matthew John Armstrong, who played Coleman's brother in the short film *Studio City*, which Coleman also wrote; Armstrong was subsequently cast as *Heroes'* radiation-spreading Ted, who at one point holds Sandra hostage while confronting Bennet. "There's like half a degree of separation," Coleman laughs. "Our lives were already intertwined before we started working together. But the *Company Man* stuff, where he's holding a gun on her – it was all so twisted and everything was so loaded, literally. That was a very odd set of scenes, where Matt Armstrong is holding a gun on his wife, who's [in character as] my wife!"

"THE WRITERS WERE VERY CAREFUL THAT THEY DIDN'T MAKE MY CHARACTER TOO VILLAINOUS, BUT IF YOU LOOK AT THE FIRST COUPLE OF EPISODES, THAT'S HOW I PLAYED HIM..."

somehow involved – how is this all going to play out? And then it comes to a head in one episode. I think it paid off wonderfully."

Away from *Heroes*, Coleman is working on producing a screenplay he's written. "The movie is a comedic drama about a young man who steals his uncle's fiancée. I'm the uncle. I'm no fool – I didn't write the lead for myself, I gave myself the third lead." Despite the enormous energy that goes into working on *Heroes*, Coleman has found inner resources for his personal project. "There's a connection and an ownership to something that you've actually created that you just can't duplicate. You become almost tireless."

Heroes fans tend to be very detail-oriented, which pleases Coleman. "Sci-fi has such loyal fans, and they're really smart. They really engage. I've never really been a sci-fi fan, but I've done enough [sci-fi] to have some experience with the fans who are and they tend to be, I think, far more attentive than your average fans. They're turned on by the specifics; the connection to the thing that they love tends to be very specific. They're paying attention. They're making connections. They're like, 'Oh, if he did this there with that person, then that must mean that he knows about this over here.' They like to connect the dots, they like the mystery. It's a pleasure to perform for them, because you know that they're paying attention to things. There are little things along the way that might be completely overlooked in a procedural show or in a soap opera, but you know [*Heroes*] fans will catch those things. It's fun for the actors, and it's fun for the writers, too. [The fans] go, 'Wait a minute, that doesn't make sense, that doesn't connect to what you said a few episodes earlier.' So you've got to be on your toes."

Heroes fans can also be very demonstrative, as Coleman discovered when he traveled to Paris

on the *Heroes* World Tour with Pasdar, Panettiere, and Ventimiglia. "We really didn't know what to expect. We knew that there was supposed to be a crowd there, and that they had advertised it. There were about seven or eight thousand people. We got out of the bus and this roar just went up. It was just surreal. It was beautiful. Everybody worked so hard on this tour, on the show, and everybody's faces were lit up."

It also provided validation of a career that has had ups and downs, Coleman believes. "It was definitely our *Hard Day's Night* moment. I remember Adrian turned to me and said, 'Not bad for a couple of old warhorses.' He and I have been around and gone through the wars and so it was just a great moment for a couple of guys in their 40s who had stuck around and refused to go away."

NAME GAME

Although the audience soon learns that Suresh's menacing taxi passenger in *Heroes*' first episode is named Noah Bennet, Coleman says, "To me, he's H.R.G. He always has been, ever since the first episode. Some people say 'Noah,' or 'Bennet,' or 'Mr. Bennet.' That all rings in my head, but H.R.G. is how he's written in the script. That's who he is."

Doesn't H.R.G. sound a bit like H.M.S., the designation of a British battleship? "Exactly," Coleman laughs. "The H.M.S. Noah Bennet!"

H.R.G. and partner-in-crime The Haitian

BAD COMPANY

A LOOK AT THE MORALLY DUBIOUS "COMPANY"

An unexpected voice in an empty apartment, a pair of horn-rimmed glasses on a desk. This is our introduction to the shadowy organization known only as "The Company."

At first, all we know is the man in the horn-rimmed glasses and his silent companion seem to be in the business of kidnapping people with special abilities, and they are trying to get their hands on Chandra Suresh's research into people with the Hero gene. Gradually, the picture widens to include other agents, both with and without abilities; secret facilities with labs, offices, and holding cells; and orders coming from some very wealthy and powerful people. One way or another, The Company seems to be behind almost everything that has gone wrong in the *Heroes* universe...

Company Man

"Dad is a bad guy, Lyle. He's a liar. Don't listen to a word he says."
"All I want is for you to have a safe and normal life."
"This isn't about me. This is all about you and the things you've done."
Claire and Mr. Bennet, *Cautionary Tales*

N oah Bennet is our entry-point into the inner workings of The Company. Like everything else about it, he is not what he seems at first. Working in the grey area between hero and villain, Mr. Bennet's career says as much about The Company as it does about him. Company loyalist Thompson recruited Mr. Bennet with the promise that he would be helping keep the world safe from people with dangerous powers. Mr. Bennet agreed that in order to do this, he was comfortable with being morally grey, and he quickly became a trusted and obedient Company man. For years, he could be counted on to carry out his assignments with ruthless efficiency, even when those assignments involved kidnapping, experimentation on human prisoners, and murder.

But secretly, his loyalty began to erode, as he rediscovered his conscience and his heart. Perhaps his conscience was stirred by the way Bob Bishop destroyed his own eight-year-old daughter Elle, testing her electrical abilities until she was permanently brain-damaged. Or perhaps it was the order to kill his partner and friend, Claude. In 14 years, he has surely been part of hundreds of disturbing incidents. No doubt at all, though, what woke Mr. Bennet's heart was his adopted daughter Claire. He knew precisely what would happen to her if he followed orders and turned her in, so he hid her abilities as long as he could. And when the secret got out in spite of him, he turned against The Company and started trying to destroy it, to save his daughter and his family.

Mr. Bennet and The Haitian

The Company has always operated like a police state. It recognizes no law, and no limit on actions its agents can take in carrying out its goal to find and control every person on Earth who has a special ability.

Angela Petrelli

Thirty Years Gone

"It all went so wrong. Thirty years ago, a group of us came together to change the world, to fix it. And Adam had a perspective on history that was compelling, and we believed in him." **Angela Petrelli,** *Powerless*

Mr. Bennet's betrayal is far from a rare exception. His Company career is a perfect parallel to the story of The Company and nearly all of its founders. In the mid-1970s, Adam Monroe brought together 12 individuals from all over the world, some with powers, some without. Their goal, as several have explained to the younger generation, was to make the world a better place. They wanted to help people with powers to learn to use them for good, and to protect the world from those whose powers were just too dangerous.

Thirty years later, all but a handful of the original founders are dead, one way or another. And scarcely anyone associated with The Company has stayed on course with his or her original intentions. Everywhere you look, there are betrayals, abrupt retirements, bitter regrets, and changes of direction and allegiance. Many of the founders lived to have nightmarish regrets about the choices that they had made, and the lives they had

ruined. When Angela and Kaito receive their death threats, both say that they deserve to die because of the pain they caused and the many people they killed.

What went wrong? Perhaps it started with the man who was The Company's inspiration. Adam Monroe, a.k.a. Takezo Kensei, had already lived for 400 years, and in that time, he had concluded that the human race was not worth saving. And he proved only the first of those who were ready to play God, putting themselves above any human standard of right and wrong.

Adam Monroe

A Brief History of The Company

Though there are many gaps in The Company's history, we can pin down a few critical dates before the fall of 2006.

- 1671: The Englishman who calls himself "Takezo Kensei" discovers that he has the power to regenerate, and swears himself to eternal enmity with the friend who betrayed him, Hiro Nakamura.

- Mid 1970s: Adam Monroe meets and recruits the original 12 to use their powers and their resources to help him save the world.

- February 14, 1977: Company biologist Victoria Pratt takes a sample of a deadly virus from Shanti Suresh and begins trying to develop a mutant strain that can be used to suppress or eliminate special abilities.

- November 2, 1977: After Adam tries to release Strain 138 into the world, Kaito Nakamura signs an order to lock him up forever. Victoria quits The Company in protest over Kaito's refusal to have Strain 138 destroyed.

- 1991: Elle Bishop, age eight, is permanently confined to the Company facility in Hartsdale, NY, after experiments with her electrical powers damage her brain and turn her into a sociopath.

- 1995: Noah Bennet is recruited into The Company by Thompson, and partnered with invisible man Claude.

- 1996: In collusion with Angela Petrelli, Kaito Nakamura gives young Claire, the illegitimate daughter of Nathan Petrelli, to Bennet to raise as his own. Soon after, Thompson sends The Haitian to erase Sandra Bennet's memory for the first time.

- 2000: Bennet is ordered to kill his partner Claude, who has begun helping people with abilities escape The Company. Claude himself escapes and literally vanishes without a trace.

- April 2006: Arthur Petrelli dies. The public story is heart attack, the story given by Angela to her sons is suicide.

- 2006: Guided by the paintings of Isaac Mendez, Daniel Linderman starts planning to ensure that Nathan Petrelli wins his congressional election, as the first step in taking charge of a post-explosion world.

With so much to hide, and so much to lose, it's no wonder that those responsible for The Company's past actions are running scared, while those still in charge continue to play as if the whole world is at stake.

Company boss Bob

Matt with The Company's Candice and Thompson

Noah Bennet in deadly action

Eden is held captive by Bennet and The Haitian

Company Policy

"People are fragile, like teacups. All around them, the world is changing and they simply don't want to deal with it. They don't want to know what's happening to us as a species."

Noah Bennet, *Company Man*

Though Company spokesmen still claim an idealistic mission, their practices, from the earliest days, fell far short of idealism. The Company has always operated like a police state. It recognizes no law, and no limit on actions its agents can take in carrying out its goal to find and control every person on Earth who has a special ability. Some of these, like Matt Parkman and West, whose abilities are under control and who have no dangerous intentions, are captured, "tagged" with a radioactive isotope, and released with their memories of their capture erased. Some with useful abilities, like Claude and Hana Gitelman, and some who are using their abilities for selfish ends, like Jessica and Eden, are offered positions in The Company. But those like Adam, Peter, and Sylar, whose abilities are dangerous and out of control, are imprisoned. And usually, The Company plans to "terminate" them as well, as Thompson plans to have Ted killed.

No matter what final disposition The Company plans for any

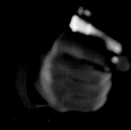

Maury Parkman

individual, it does one thing to everyone: Company scientists study each ability, to find its limits, learn how it works and perhaps most importantly, to determine ways to control it and the individual in case they ever become dangerous. Even 30 years ago, The Company's scientific resources must have been extraordinary. It took Victoria Pratt and her team of biologists only a few months to develop many mutations of the Shanti virus, all intended to help suppress abilities; and one so deadly it could wipe out the human race. Yet with all their resources, The Company still hasn't achieved the simplest and most humane of goals: a way to switch off the Hero mutation, permanently and safely. After Adam first tried to release Strain 138, The Company had good reason to suspend, for decades, the research on the Shanti virus. Yet there is no hint that they explored other avenues of genetics and biochemistry in search of a cure. Perhaps those in charge, like Linderman and Bob Bishop, have their own reasons for not wanting to find one.

Claude the "invisible man"

The Faces in the Photograph

The 12 original founders of The Company, as seen in the group photo Matt Parkman uses to try to locate them.

Kaito Nakamura: Power unknown. Murdered by Adam Monroe.
Charles Deveaux: Power unknown. Died of natural causes.
Arthur Petrelli: Power unknown. Died of unknown causes.
Daniel Linderman: Healer. Killed by D.L. Hawkins in self-defense.
Angela Petrelli: Power unknown. Living.
Maury Parkman: Telepath. Living; in Company custody.
Bob Bishop: Transmutation. Living; currently head of The Company.
Victoria Pratt: Power unknown. Murdered by Adam Monroe.
Paula Gramble: Power unknown. Deceased, no details.
Harry Fletcher: Power unknown. Deceased, no details.
Susan Ammaw: Power unknown. Deceased, no details.
Carlos Mendez: Power unknown. Deceased, no details.

Not in group photo: Adam Monroe. Regeneration. Buried alive by Hiro Nakamura.

One of Us, One of Them

"Is it true? Are you hiding one of them?"
"By 'them', do you mean people like me? Is that what you're accusing me of hiding? Well, the short answer's yes, isn't it?"
"You compromised what we're doing."
"Sorry. I mean, I know we're serving the greater good, but the vivisection started to keep me up at night. Seeing as you're raising one of us as your own, I was hoping for a bit more sympathy."
Mr. Bennet and Claude, *Company Man*

The Company's founders were a mix of people with abilities and people without. It's not surprising, then, that their whole organization is structured along the same lines. Their agents work in pairs, and as Thompson explains to the newly recruited Bennet, the pairs are always made up of a normal human, and a human with a special ability. Those with special abilities are, of course, very useful in Company operations, especially when they can do things that give a decisive advantage over others. The higher-ups recognized immediately the potential of people like The Haitian and Eden, and they're very interested in Matt Parkman's telepathy as well.

With those special abilities being so valued in field operations, why doesn't The Company ever partner two agents with special abilities? You'd expect, in an organization founded partly by people with special abilities, that gifted pairs might be specially valued or trusted. But the gifted agents, like The Haitian, Eden, and Candice, often seem

Bennet and The Haitian watch their captive, Sylar

to be under the orders of their normal partners. According to Thompson, The Company thinks that the Heroes need someone to keep an eye on them, and keep their powers under control.

If The Company sees those with special abilities as a high risk, they have good reason. Virtually every gifted Company agent we've seen has eventually become a problem. Claude turned against The Company after years of watching them experiment on people just like him. Eden helped Mr. Bennet hide Claire's ability, proving that her loyalty, too, belonged to helping her own kind before The Company. And The Haitian's loyalty seems to belong to almost anyone but The Company; he has helped Mr. Bennet hide Claire, helped Claire and Angela Petrelli keep secrets from Mr. Bennet and The Company, and finally, on his own, hid Peter Petrelli from everyone, including Angela.

Everything to Hide

"They killed Dad. They're never going to leave us alone."
"You do realize what'll happen to us if you tell everyone what you can do."
"Yes. No more running. No more hiding. No more secrets."
Claire and Sandra Bennet, *Powerless*

One of The Company's key doctrines is secrecy: the public must never discover the existence of people with special abilities. To that end they not only capture everyone they can find with special abilities, but they will go to any lengths, including erasing memories, destroying records, and even assassination, to stop anyone from revealing their powers. The real question is, why? Of course one could argue, quite reasonably, that public knowledge would lead to public hysteria and persecution of people with abilities. People like Sylar, Ted, and Maya would give the public good cause to fear. On the other hand, we have seen just as many Heroes who use their abilities to help the world, and whose work could be used to do good.

No Company agent has ever spelled out a good reason for this secrecy. And they don't need to. Their own practices are more than enough justification. Public fears of people with special abilities would be insignificant beside the public hysteria over an organization responsible for hundreds of secret kidnappings, experiments, even vivisections, and murders. And if the news was leaked that Company experiments had created a virus so deadly it could kill every human on Earth, the response would be catastrophic. Every government in the world would descend on The Company, with wholesale arrests, investigations, public hearings, and, almost certainly, secret attempts to get control of The Company's arsenal and its scientific resources.

With so much to hide, and so much to lose, it's no wonder that those responsible for The Company's past actions are running scared, while those still in charge continue to play as if the whole world is at stake. For them and for the good guys, it is.

Mr. Linderman

The Haitian

Unanswered Questions

There are many gaps in the history of The Company apart from the complete lack of any information about most of its founders. A few of the most intriguing questions at the end of season two include...

After The Company located Shanti Suresh and harvested a sample of the virus from her, did they have any relationship with Chandra, or keep track of his work, during the next 30 years?

Who in The Company told Adam about Strain 138 and what it could do?

What were The Company's real reasons for refusing to destroy all samples of Strain 138?

Is there any relationship between Isaac Mendez and Company founder Carlos Mendez?

How did Arthur Petrelli really die? Did he commit suicide, as Angela tells her sons, or was he another murder victim?

Why did The Company order Mr. Bennet to keep Sylar alive after *Homecoming*, despite all evidence that he was extremely dangerous?

What else is in The Company's top-security vault in Odessa?

Given Adam's history, why was Kaito so surprised that Adam was his murderer?

Why was Maury Parkman working with Adam to eliminate the other Founders?

Who ordered the assassination of Nathan? How did they find out what he was going to reveal at his press conference? And did Angela know about the attack on her own son, before it happened?

The Company's Thompson

Heroes and Villains

Heroes creator Tim Kring takes time out of his super-busy schedule to talk about the critics' reaction to season two and to exclusively preview season three – and volume three, *Villains*…

It's not all fun and games being the mastermind behind a massive television show like *Heroes*. For all the joys that come with wounding the immortal Claire in several nasty ways or sending Hiro to Feudal Japan, it's certainly tempered by the criticism from the audience, the ridiculously long hours behind the scenes, and even the dreaded writer's block. You have to *really* adore what you're doing to get through the grind of the TV machine – and there's no question that *Heroes* creator and show-runner Tim Kring feels that way about his latest gig.

On any given day, he's plotting out the latest adventures of the Petrelli clan, the evil machinations of The Company, or the upcoming volume called *Villains*. It doesn't get much cooler than that. Even coming off a strike-shortened sophomore season that was heavily criticized, Kring is frank about both the positives and negatives of his job.

"Making a television show is a very imperfect and imprecise science," Kring admits from his office in Hollywood. "Any creative endeavor is." He even addressed that fact publicly in *Entertainment Weekly* last year where he assessed some flaws in the second season – a rather gutsy move in a medium where aversion is commonplace.

Kring just chuckles, "I was asked a question by a reporter which was, 'Would you do anything different?' The truth is that the way I work, and I think also for most people who work in a medium like this with such financial constraints and time constraints, if I am asked the question 'would I do anything different?', the answer is always, 'Are you kidding?! Everything!' Every time you go onto the set, it's not exactly what you pictured in your mind. You always have to make 50 compromises which don't

Photo: Albert Ortega

This spread:
Tim Kring (above);
Villains like Sylar and
Adam Monroe are set
to take center-stage;
Also, season three is
set to focus on the
Petrelli clan...
Overleaf: Will Matt
Parkman's villainous
father return...?

make you completely happy. 'Maybe I shouldn't have painted that wall blue and why is that guy's hair parted on the side?' You try things and some things work and some don't. There are a million different things, and we are all perfectionists over here so we want to make the best show we can. Nobody ever asked me that question in the first season, but I would have answered the same way.

"In the second season, I think we had some interesting things happen," Kring continues regarding the *Generations* criticisms. "You can't really plan for the audience's reaction to things, and one of the things we found out was that the audience did not want to start slowly and build. But sure enough, that happened in the first season and I think people don't really remember that. When I logged onto chatrooms in the first season, during episodes seven and eight, it was really depressing because the fans were just livid. They said, 'This isn't making any

sense! The characters haven't come together, nothing is happening!' Three episodes later, when I logged on we were suddenly doing everything right!"

Yet, on the other hand, a huge factor that Kring had little control over in season two was its abrupt end due to the writers' strike, which shut down production for 100 days. "Thankfully, we air our show in volumes and not in seasons," Kring relates. "The audience hasn't really gotten used to that idea; although they would have had we had a whole second season. The second season was going to be three separate volumes. The second volume was always intended to end at episode 11, so when we literally got to the strike we were filming the finale of that volume – *Generations*. Fortunately and coincidentally, we were able to wrap up that volume completely so that it could, in a weird way, stand on its own as a second season with a beginning, middle, and an end. It was just a stroke of luck that the strike just happened to fall then. Had it fallen eight episodes in or

"I think *Villains* is going to be a fan favorite. It hits the ground extremely aggressively."

16 episodes into the season, we would have been halfway through the next volume. It was a fortunate thing."

While it worked out, Kring does admit there was a lot of disappointment internally that they had to scrap so much completed scripting. "We had put a lot of work into the volume," he sighs. "We were already planning episode 16 at the time, and we shot almost two episodes worth of material that will only be seen in the season two *Heroes* DVD – which is the Holy Grail of DVD features! It's something that won't be seen in any other way. So yes, it was a very difficult decision to make, but it was really the right decision to make. We asked ourselves a very important question and that was: 'If the end of *Generations* was going to be, to all effects, the end of season two, could episode 12 – the beginning of the next volume – stand alone as a season opener nine months later?' We looked at each other and we looked at that episode and said, 'No way!' No way was

it a season opener – it would kill us! It was too connected to the other story and too serialized and hard to understand. It would have been a bad situation if we were on strike for six months and that's how we came back. So that was the hard decision that made us do this, but it was exactly the right one to do. Had the strike been three weeks, we would have had to rethink things, but it was a long strike and then we did not come back, so we'll have been off the air for nine months. We needed a real re-launch."

The long winter break, despite how difficult it was for the industry overall, did provide the writers with something quite rare – a break from the creative grind of the show. "It was a huge positive in that regard," Kring shares. "The silver lining of the strike was the time away from the show so we could assess all the things that had worked and didn't work. People watched season one and then took a break off of it for three or four months then came back and watched season two. That's not our experience. We took less than a week off in between. People ask, why isn't season two like season one? Why is it different? For us it was all the same – one big, long blur with the same writers, actors, same directors, producers, same story-breaking techniques, and the same discussions. We basically just

"The silver lining of the strike was the time away from the show to assess all the things that had worked and didn't work."

went home for a couple days and came back, so for us there was really no break.

"In any creative endeavor, you just need to be able to step back and look at what it is that you are doing," he continues. "It's like a painter who paints a canvas and has to step back to the other side of the room and look at it every once in awhile. It really allowed me personally to assess things and ask some very hard questions and some very obvious questions. I think, because of that, this volume, *Villains*, is going to be a fan favorite."

Specifically, Kring says the hiatus allowed the writing team to jump-start the pace of the show. "Attention spans change when the audience gets used to a certain amount of adrenaline in the storyline, so that's what we've corrected in the third volume," he details. "It hits the ground extremely aggressively and tells the story in an aggressive way. Plus, the morale couldn't be higher and the scripts couldn't be better and the show couldn't look any better and that's all because of the break."

So just what can fans expect from such an ominously loaded title such as *Villains*? We know Sylar is back in action from the epilogue of *Generations*, but what other evil is afoot? Kring smiles and says, "*Villains* refers as much to our own characters as the added characters in the show. It's as much about the dichotomy of all of us – that inside of us we have the good and the bad, the heroic and the villainous. That in many ways is at the heart of this as all of our characters will be tested in ways that will call into question what their core values are really about.

"That being said, we are unleashing onto the world a little cadre of villains," he teases with glee. "We have introduced the idea of a Company facility where many of these people have been housed and 'bagged and tagged.' Let's just say that several of them find their way out into the real world and have to be contained again."

Maybe just as importantly, Kring says this volume allows him to get back to some important threads left dangling from season one. "There were several key questions that the first season asked, and they were very primal questions. The questions were things like: 'Who am I?' 'What is happening to me?' 'How am I connected to other people?' and 'Where are these powers coming from?' Those questions were very primal, very archetypal questions. In many ways, as we went farther and farther into the show and into volume two, those questions became less important, but I don't think they are less important to the audience. I'll just say that *Villains* takes all those questions and reframes them and asks them in a new way."

Pretty exciting stuff, especially when it comes to the characters that will be acting all of this drama out week after week. Kring says all of the core cast will get some time to shine in this story arc. "The show has always been very much about families and dynasties, which is what *Generations* is about," he details. "It's about the previous generation and the sins of the parents visited upon the children. When we get to volume three, we dig much farther into that, and the Petrelli dynasty takes on a whole new level of intensity. But the familial stuff with our other characters, like Matt Parkman and his father; Claire and the Bennet family; Hiro and his legacy from his father – all of those things are really still alive and percolating. Yet the Petrelli family becomes front and center for much of the plot. It's very cool and anybody who loves that idea will get their money's worth in the next volume." ☼